Introduction

This book will introduce you to some of the greatest Christians who have ever lived. Although they were persecuted by a brutal regime, the sheer quality of their lives overcame all opposition. In the end, even some of their persecutors were convinced and converted. They "turned the world upside down."

These Christians lacked many of the things we consider essential to Christian activity—printed Bibles and other books, visual aids, electric organs, visitation programs and even, in most cases, church buildings. Yet they succeeded in evangelizing the known world. They had no Bible colleges, no cathedrals, no mission societies nor schools, no influential friends in the Administration. But they had an irresistible belief in the truth of their message and an unshakable faith in the power and authority of the Lord Jesus Christ.

It is sad that few modern Christians know even the names of these men, who are their spiritual forefathers. Polycarp, Cyprian, Athanasius, Irenaeus, Justin, Clement, Ignatius—names such as theirs are not nearly as familiar to us as such New Testament characters as Peter, Paul, John, Mark and Timothy. Yet they were their immediate successors. Some of them were born during the lifetime of the apostles, and grew up in the heady atmosphere of the apostolic Church.

Some came in the second and third centuries A.D., spiritual giants who guided the infant Church through the period when the New Testament documents were slowly being collated and accepted as Scripture. They fought to keep the faith pure against all manner of heresies and distortions. They battled to keep the Church alive when the authorities went to appalling lengths to wipe it out completely. They courageously carried the Gospel to the farthest corners of the Roman Empire, and beyond. And they succeeded in winning that Empire for Christ.

Surely men (and women) like these deserve to be known and remembered—especially through their own letters and other writings! The Church of the first two or three centuries is the closest thing history has known to a united Church. What is more, it is that Church which is the mother of us all—Episcopalians, Presbyterians, Independents, Baptists, Catholics: all agree that this was the true Church, the one Christ founded. So, looking at that Church, and at its leaders and members, is like looking into a picture of the Church as Christ wanted it to be. The experience is disturbing and challenging, but I do not believe anyone can read the words of these "early Church Fathers" without having his faith and vision renewed.

Of course, even the early Church was not perfect, nor its leaders infallible.[1] In reading their words you may permit yourself a luxury denied us when we read the Bible, the luxury of disagreeing with them, if you wish! They seem, to modern eyes, somewhat obsessed with church order, somewhat unyielding over church discipline. Heretics of any kind get short shrift from them. There are many appeals to Christians to submit to their elders, to "toe the line."

But in their situation, this was reasonable. Without, as yet, a universally accepted New Testament, and with only an embryonic form of church government, they were desperately aware of the danger of the church splitting into a thousand warring fragments. Yet in spite of these lacks they maintained unity, and the world believed.

Most of the writers quoted in this book lived in the period from about A.D. 70-300. The most "modern" of them is the great Augustine of Hippo, who lived from A.D. 354-430. The "oldest" of them is probably the anonymous writer of the "Didache" (the "Teaching"), which is as old as parts of the New Testament. So the readings cover the vital, formative years of Christianity, from apostolic times to the point at which Christianity had become the dominant religion of the Roman world.

Studying these writings, as I have done in compiling this

100 DAYS
IN THE ARENA

One hundred dynamic readings
from great men
of the early church,
paraphrased for today

BY DAVID WINTER

Harold Shaw Publishers
Wheaton, Illinois

Library of Congress Catalog Card Number 77-92353
ISBN 0-87788-270-3

Printed in the United States of America

book, is a strange experience. Literally and spiritually, the lives of these early Christians were spent "in the arena". They faced political and supernatural powers as dangerous as the lions which were loosed on them in the Coliseum. In some ways this was a Church quite unlike anything we know today. Its cultural setting, its intensity of worship, its pervading atmosphere of the miraculous, its incredible courage in the face of persecution—few of us can claim to have experienced anything like it.

In other ways, it is very like the Church of today. The problems of the Christian life do not seem to have changed very much. Like us, these early Christians worried about their besetting sins. They wondered how to win unbelievers to Christ. They grappled with dissension in the Church, troubles in the family and rebellious adolescents. These are not demi-gods from another world, but men and women like ourselves, though (I dare to suggest) nearer to the source of grace, closer to Christ, more open to the Spirit than most of us.

The early Church also offers, to modern eyes, a strange contradiction of our usual assumptions about "labels." At one moment it seems very "catholic," at another very "protestant." Quite a few of my long-cherished prejudices took a knock at the hands of these Christians of long ago, rebuking the way in which I had categorized my fellow Christians of today. The fact is that all of our traditions began and had their roots in this most fertile soil. It is like looking at an old family photo album and recognizing the family features in those fading portraits from the past.

Reading the words of these Christians from nineteen centuries ago has done two things for me, and I hope it will do the same for those who share my experience.

It has given me a new pride in the Church founded by the Lord Jesus Christ. With ancestors like these, none of us needs be ashamed of the Church of which he is a member today. I cannot think of any people in any age who exhibited more clearly all the things we most admire: courage, consistency, love, faith, generosity... but above all, courage. These people were heroes and heroines whose bravery simply defies description.

The second thing relates to the New Testament. For many of us our Christian reading stops at the end of Revelation and picks up again around the time of D. L. Moody, C. H. Spurgeon or even C. S. Lewis. Little wonder, then, that at times the New Testament seems a somewhat remote, distant book, a jewel without a setting, a picture of a distant Utopia far removed from ordinary life.

But when I started to read the letters and documents of these early Christians, my view of the New Testament changed. I had a new angle on it. Now it was not a text-book suspended in historical space, spelling out a message to me across the dividing centuries, but an intensely human document. I had come to know the people for whom, historically speaking, it was written. I had sensed the "feel" of the era when the inspired Word of the New Testament was collated, recognized and accepted as Holy Scripture, on a level with the Old Testament as part of God's unique revelation to mankind.

Suddenly I saw that it was not something detached from its setting, but it was truly the jewel set in the middle of a whole sea of similar writings—similar in style and content and message, though lacking that direct authority of the apostles (and through them, of Christ) which distinguishes the inspired Word of God from the inspiring words of men.

I have paraphrased their words with some freedom, while keeping meticulously to the basic ideas and concepts they expressed. But translated and paraphrased into our modern idiom, these words *are* still inspiring, and they are part of *our* heritage. The writers are our brothers and sisters in Christ. Their battles are our battles. Their Enemy is our Enemy. Their arena of life is also ours, as is their conquering faith. In fact, the Church we will glimpse in these pages, for all that it is separated from us by nearly two millenia, is *our* Church, with Christ as its victorious Head.

David Winter

---

[1]*Indeed, one or two of the writers quoted are, or have been, regarded as unorthodox in certain of their views—though not in the passages quoted!*

The Writers

Clement of Rome
Clement is undoubtedly one of the earliest Christian writers after the apostles. His letter to the church at Corinth was almost certainly written during the last decade of the first century—in other words, within a lifetime of the Resurrection.

He was probably bishop of the church at Rome, though one ought to add that his role was not necessarily that of a modern bishop. He was the *overseer* of the church in that city, and had guided it through times of serious persecution under Domitian.

His letter resulted from news reaching Rome of trouble in the church at Corinth, where some completely innocent presbyters had been put out of office. Clearly the church in Rome was distressed to hear of this dissension in a sister church, and Clement's letter is a call to them to maintain the unity of the faith.

Judging from this letter, the Roman church was a mature, well-balanced community, though not notable for charismatic gifts, nor for any preoccupation with an imminent Second Coming. Clement himself was a man who saw in vivid terms the distinction between a world in darkness and the people of God, lit with the light of Christ.

Ignatius
Ignatius was probably converted in adult life, and eventually he became bishop of the church at Antioch. Condemned to death for his faith, he was taken on the long journey to Rome escorted by Roman soldiers, expecting to be thrown to wild beasts in the arena.

During this journey he was able to write several letters to

churches along or near his route, and it is these which still survive and from which we quote in this book.

Eventually, Ignatius was martyred in Rome, probably in the year 107.

His letters show us his intensity and passion—not surprising, in view of the circumstances in which they were written. He was almost obsessively concerned with defending the unity of the church and the authority of the bishop, whom he saw as the only guarantor of that unity. But he was also utterly devoted to Christ, and expressed that devotion in terms that speak as convincingly to the modern reader as they must have done to his contemporaries.

Polycarp
Polycarp is an important link between the apostolic age and the Church of the second century. Irenaeus says that Polycarp was instructed by the apostle John himself. This fact later lent great authority to his position as bishop of Smyrna, where he suffered martyrdom in about 155 A.D.

Justin
Justin's arguments in defense of the divine origin and authority of Christianity made him an important second-century Christian apologist. Born in Samaria of pagan parents, he became a Christian after many years of studying philosophy. He later sought to show that Christianity did not conflict with the best Greek philosophy. After teaching for a while in Ephesus he opened a Christian school in Rome. His *First and Second Apology* and his *Dialogue with Trypho* survive, and court records give an account of his martyrdom.

Irenaeus
Irenaeus was born in Asia Minor about 130, but most of his ministry was spent in Gaul (modern France). He eventually became bishop of Lyons and died, possibly a martyr, in the early years of the next century.

Most of his writing is directed against the heresy known as *gnosticism*. This claimed secret revelations which turned the Christian doctrine of the Incarnation (that Christ was both divine and human) into a purely "spiritual" notion. Irenaeus saw that such ideas would eventually turn the Christian gospel into an exercise in Greek philosophy, and he argued with great authority that God had revealed himself uniquely and finally in the person and work of Christ.

Tertullian

Tertullian was born in Carthage about the year 160. He was a well-educated lawyer, probably living in Rome, where he was converted to Christianity. Leaving behind a life of licentiousness, he returned to North Africa and became a teacher of Christian doctrine, writing many essays for both Christians and non-Christians. He was attracted to the Montanists because of their strict moral standards, joining the group in about 207. Later he founded an even more ascetic party of his own, which was denounced for its extreme legalism. However, in most respects he remained orthodox in his beliefs and made important contributions to the doctrine of the Trinity (we owe the word "Trinity" to him) and to our understanding of the person and work of Jesus.

Clement of Alexandria

Clement was the last and greatest of the second century apologists. He succeeded his teacher Pantaemis as head of a school for the instruction of converts at Alexandria, and was succeeded by his pupil Origen. He attempted to accommodate Christianity to Greek culture, maintaining that philosophy was for the Greeks, (as the Law of Moses was for the Jews) a schoolmaster leading to Christ. He opposed Gnosticism, a heresy which denied the humanity of Jesus, by maintaining that the only true "gnosis" or spiritual knowledge was to be found in the orthodox Christian faith.

Origen

Origen is the first of these leaders to have been born into a Christian home. In fact, his father died for the faith in A.D. 203. He is also distinguished by the fact that he spent much of his life as a layman, as the head of a Christian school in Alexandria. In fact, he took on the headship at the age of eighteen, when the great

Clement of Alexandria retired. While still a young man he was invited to expound the Scriptures to the bishops of Palestine—an unusual distinction for a layman in those days.

He ran into trouble later in his life, was accused of doctrinal errors and was ordained by the bishops of Caesarea and Jerusalem, without the permission of his own bishop. As a result of this rift he made Caesarea his home, and turned out a stream of doctrinal books and biblical commentaries.

He died in 254, his death hastened by torture which he suffered during the Decian persecution.

Cyprian

Cyprian was a distinguished lawyer before his conversion in 246. A wealthy nobleman, he rapidly gained acceptance in the church after his baptism, and became bishop of the church in Carthage and a leading Christian statesman. He went into hiding during the Decian persecution, but reappeared to deal—rather harshly—with the problem of Christians who had denied Christ during that period and now wished to be reinstated.

Aphraates

Aphraates, known as the "Persian Sage," may have been a bishop and martyr. Between 336 and 345 he wrote 23 theological treatises, usually called "homilies," which reflect the asceticism of the East Syrian Church and express a view of God largely uninfluenced by Greek thought.

Ephraem

Ephraem, or Ephrem Syrus (i.e., the Syrian) was a voluminous writer, mostly in verse, of expositions of Scripture, refutations of heresies, hymns, and ascetic writings. He became famous for his learning and his austere life-style. He may have attended the Council of Nicaea in 325.

Athanasius

Athanasius was the great opponent of Arianism, a heresy which was the greatest single threat to the church in the fourth century. He insisted upon the doctrine of the full deity and manhood of Christ, the Son, as opposed to the Arian view that the Christ was a creature, and not the only begotten Son of God. The great Athanasian Creed is named in his honor. Athansius was bishop of Alexandria from 328 to 373, but during this time he suffered exile five times because of the political intrigues of the Arian party.

John Chrysostom

John, called "Chrysostom" ("golden mouthed") because of his eloquence, was a native of Antioch, where he became an elder and a renowned preacher. He excelled as an expositor of Scripture, rejecting the allegorical method of interpretation and insisting on a literal exegesis. In 397, much against his will, he was made bishop of Constantinople. He became popular with the common people, but fell into disfavor at the imperial court, partly through the hostility of Theophilus, the influential bishop of Alexandria, and partly because of the displeasure of the Empress Eudoria, whom he compared to Herodias (see Mark 6:17-28). He was banished in 403, recalled briefly on account of his popularity, but soon banished again, and died in exile in 407. A large number of his sermons, treatises, and letters have come down to us—more than from any other of the Greek fathers.

Augustine

Augustine is one of the most important figures in the history of the church, as well as being eminent in the history of European philosophy and literature. He was born in North Africa in 354. Though his mother, Monica, was a Christian, and though he received a Christian education, he was for some years an adherent of a false cult known as Manichaeism. After studying rhetoric in Carthage, he went to teach in Rome and then in Milan, where he came under the influence of the bishop, Ambrose. His conversion came about through reading Romans 13:13, 14, and he was baptized on Easter Eve in 387. The story of his early life and conversion is told in his classic *Confessions*, whose theme is expressed in the famous words, "Thou has made us for Thyself and our heart is restless until it rests in Thee." Returning to North Africa, he entered the monastic life, was later ordained, and in 396 became bishop of Hippo, remaining so till his death in 430.

Many of his writings are polemical, concerned with three

heresies which he regarded as major threats to the church: Manichaeism, which denied the Resurrection and held that the material universe was evil, Donatism, with its legalistic asceticism, and Pelagianism which denied original sin and affirmed the possibility of a sinless life for believers. Besides his *Confessions*, his most famous work is *The City of God*, in which he develops an understanding of history based on the conflict between the two "cities", the city of God, and the city of the world.

Hermas

Hermas is known only as the author of *The Shepherd*, which derived its name from the "angel of repentance" who appeared to Hermas in visions in the guise of a shepherd. The book is concerned with the question of whether sins committed after baptism could be forgiven. It was highly esteemed in the second and third centuries, especially in the eastern church, some even regarding it on a level with Scripture.

Unknown Authorship

Three of the selections are of unknown authorship. The *Didache* and the *Epistle of Barnabas* are usually assigned to the late first or early second century. The *Epistle of Diognetus* is thought to belong to the second or third century.

The *Didache* (Greek for "Teaching") has as its full title *The Teaching of the Lord Through the Twelve Apostles to the Gentiles*. It begins with an exhortation on "the two ways"—the way of life and the way of death—and goes on to give regulations regarding the administration of baptism and the eucharist, the recognition of prophets, and other matters of church order.

The *Epistle of Barnabas* sets forth an allegorical interpretation of passages of the Old Testament, finding in them predictions regarding Christ. It maintains that the Jews misinterpreted the ceremonial law in taking it literally and setting up a material temple and animal sacrifices.

The *Epistle to Diognetus* is an apologetic work attacking pagan idolatry and Jewish sacrifices and describing Christians as strangers and pilgrims whose citizenship is in heaven. Its account of redemption reflects the Pauline doctrine of grace.

Heaven and earth cannot contain you... any more than my small heart can

How shall I pray to God—my God, my Lord? It seems strange to ask him to "come into my heart." After all, he is the God who made the heavens and the earth, and the Bible tells me that even they cannot contain him. So how can my poor, small heart invite him in?

And yet we also read that you are present in all things, Lord. Without you, nothing that is can exist. You "fill all things:" every place, high or low; heaven and the grave; light and darkness; the "uttermost parts of the sea." Nothing exists without you. Nothing can exclude you.

Surely that means that even I cannot exclude you; that if you were not in me, nor I in you, I should not exist.

Which leaves two mysteries: how can the infinite God of heaven and earth enter my small heart? And, how can I ask him in, *who is already there?*

Of course, heaven and earth cannot *contain* you, the Infinite One, any more than my small heart can. There can be no limits, no boundaries to confine one who "fills everything." But to say you are everywhere, Lord, is not to say that everywhere has all of you. We say a bucket is "full" of water, but it contains only a drop compared with rivers and lakes and oceans. Though you fill all things, you do not necessarily give them all of yourself.

But I can pray truly that my heart, where you already have a foothold, may receive more and more of you, until one day the whole of me will be filled with the whole of you.

Augustine of Hippo (354-430 A.D.)

The door to repentance is always open

If we are ever tempted to feel that it is too late for us to repent, or that we have persisted in sin for so long that we have exhausted God's patience with us, we should remember two things.

The first is that in every generation the Lord has offered the chance of repentance to anybody who turns to him. This has been true since the days of Noah, when those who took notice of his warnings and repented were saved. Centuries later, the people of Nineveh repented when Jonah warned them of God's judgment. Although they were not his people, they turned to God with prayer and pleaded for forgiveness—and they received it.

The constant message of our teachers, through the Holy Spirit, is repentance. "By my oath," the Lord himself declares, "I do not want the sinner to die, but to repent." And in another part of Scripture he says, "Though your sins are red as crimson, I will make them as white as snow".

So it is God's own will that every one of his dear children should find that the door to repentance is always open. And when we enter it, we shall find how precious is the blood of Christ in God's eyes. For it is that blood, poured out for our forgiveness, that offers grace to all mankind.

Clement of Rome (30-100 A.D.)

We can say "our bread" because it is food for those who are united to Christ

"Give us this day our daily bread." And he does, in two senses: our food, which sustains our bodies, and his Son, who sustains our spirits. For Christ is the bread of life, a bread which belongs to those who are his. We say *"Our* Father," because he is the Father of those who are his sons; and we say *"our* bread," because it is food for those who are united to Christ.

So, just as we need our daily food, and cannot survive without it, we ask also for our spiritual food each day. We remember that Christ said, "I am the bread of life come down from heaven. If anyone eats this bread, he will live for ever; and that bread—the bread I give—is my flesh, offered for the life of the world." And he also warns, "Unless you eat the flesh of the Son of Man, and drink his blood, you have no life in you."

The promise, and the warning, are vividly expressed in the bread we break at the communion table. We receive it as heavenly bread, assured that we shall "live for ever." But to deprive ourselves of it, or to be cut off from it by our sin or disobedience, is to cut ourselves off from that same life. For to be separated from Christ is to be separated from life itself.

So we ask that every day we may be given our daily bread (that is, Christ) so that we who live in him may be strengthened and made holy.

Cyprian (200-258 A.D.)

You give yourself with such generosity, it might almost seem that you need us

Child of Bethlehem, what contrasts you embrace! No one has ever been so humble; no one has ever wielded such power. We stand in awe of your holiness, and yet we are bathed in your love.

And where shall we look for you? You are in high heaven, in the glory of the Godhead. Yet those who searched for you on earth found you in a tiny baby at Mary's breast. We come in hushed reverence to find you as God, and you welcome us as man. We come unthinkingly to find you as man, and are blinded by the light of your Godhead.

You are the heir to King David's throne, but you renounced all of his royal splendor. Of all his luxurious bedrooms, you chose a stable. Of all his magnificent beds, you chose a feeding-trough. Of all his golden chariots, you chose an ass.

Never was there a king like you! Instead of royal isolation, you made yourself available to everyone who needed you. Instead of high security, you made yourself vulnerable to those who hated you.

It is we who need you, above anything in the world. You give yourself to us with such total generosity, that it might almost seem that you need us. There never was a king like this before!

Ephraem of Syria (300-379 A.D.)

Christians are nationals of various states, but citizens of heaven

You can't tell a Christian from a non-Christian by where he lives, or the way he speaks or how he dresses. There are no "Christian towns," there is no "Christian language," and they eat, drink and sleep just like everybody else. Christians aren't particularly clever or ingenious, and they haven't mastered some complicated formula, like the followers of some religions.

But, while it's true that they live in cities next to other people, and follow the same pattern of life as they do, in fact they have a unique citizenship of their own. They are, of course, citizens of their own lands—loyal ones, too. But yet they feel like visitors. Every foreign country is their homeland, and their homeland is like a foreign country to them.

Epistle to Diognetus (c. 150 A.D.)

Your weapon of attack is nothing but love

In the process of learning—which is what the Christian life really is—we all need to work together. Sometimes we will wrestle together with some problem; sometimes we will race together towards a common objective. We share the same anxieties and disappointments; we share the same moments of tranquility as we rest in the Lord, and the same moments when we are called together to rise to some new challenge. We are all members of God's household—his stewards, his assistants, his servants.

Or, if you prefer, we are soldiers of his army, in the pay of a commander whom we are called to satisfy by our service. Let there be no deserters from his ranks! Your baptism is a shield and your faith a helmet to protect you, and your patient endurance is like the armor around your body. Your weapon of attack is nothing but love.

You know how soldiers put their pay into a savings account, so that one day they can draw out what they have earned. Let us learn from them, and lay up a deposit of good actions, of kind deeds, which on "that day" we will be able to draw upon in heaven.

Ignatius of Antioch (c. 35-c.107 A.D.)

Denying yourself good things is no road to holiness

I was sitting on a hillside, rather pleased with myself. I was fasting, as I often did, denying myself food, and getting up very early to climb the mountain and pray. I felt in this way I could repay the Lord for some of the difficult things he went through for me.

But then the shepherd approached me.

"What are you doing up here so early in the morning?" he asked.

"I'm observing a fast," I said, "to the Lord."

"What sort of a fast is that?"

"Oh, my usual. I abstain from food. Deny myself luxuries. Get up early. And pray."

The shepherd didn't look impressed.

"That's not the sort of fast that pleases the Lord," he said. "That's not what he asks of you."

He could see the puzzled look on my face.

"Look, God does not want you to deny yourself *good* things. That is no road to holiness. A true fast is to deny yourself *bad* things: keep his commandments, do what he says, reject evil thoughts and desires the moment they enter your imagination. Reject what is wrong and serve God with a simple, uncomplicated heart. If you do that, you are fasting—fasting in a way that pleases the Lord."

The Shepherd of Hermas (2nd century A.D.)

It is faith that saves us from the flood tide of fear

It is faith that lifts us up to heaven. It is faith that saves us from the flood tide of fear. It is faith that sets us free from our prisons, extinguishes the burning fire that threatens us, feeds us when we are hungry, raises us from death and makes nobodies into somebodies.

    And what is this faith?

    It is believing that God is Lord of all.

    That he made the earth, the sky and the seas,
        and everything in them.

    That he made man in his own image.

    That he gave the law to Moses and his Spirit to
        the prophets.

    That he sent the Messiah, Jesus, into the
        world, to give life to those who were dying.

    It is believing in this and being baptized
        in these beliefs.

    This is that faith.

Aphraates of Persia (4th century A.D.)

Faith is not only believing. It is also denying sin.

Faith saves and rescues us, as we believe in God and in Christ; in the glory of the Lord of all and the love of the Savior of all. Faith is believing in these things.

    Faith is not *only* believing, however. It is also
        denying:
    Denying superstition, and the observing of
        special days and seasons, and the use
        of astrology, magic and spells.
    Denying immorality, self-indulgence and satanism.
    Denying flattery, blasphemy and disloyalty.
    Denying lies and deceitful words.
    This is that faith: built on a rock—the Rock,
        the Lord Jesus, upon whom alone we can build to last.

Aphraates of Persia (4th century A.D.)

Envy and jealousy are nothing but self-induced fantasies

Jealousy and envy have often caused havoc, even in the Church, and some of our most godly leaders have suffered because of it.

Look at the apostles. Peter was the object of sinful jealousy on several occasions. So was Paul, who because of the jealousy and envy of others, was arrested several times, imprisoned, stoned, exiled. He did not let this distract him from his ministry. Disregarding the envy of lesser people, he preached the Gospel all over the world, made his testimony in front of kings and rulers, and in the end silenced the critics by his faith, his patience and his endurance.

But it's not only the famous who suffer through envy. Plenty of ordinary Christians have gone through agony because others have envied their courage and confidence.

For example, there were those brave Christian women, here in Rome, who were hounded by unbelievers who resented their peace and joy in believing. Out of sheer envy, their enemies tried to make them act the parts of pagan goddesses in heathen rituals; and when they refused, they were shamefully put to death.

Jealousy has divided homes. It has come between husbands and wives, contradicting the Bible's claim that a wife is bone of her husband's bone, and flesh of his flesh. Envy and jealousy have brought ruin to prosperous cities and overthrown great nations.

So, let's remind ourselves that envy and jealousy are nothing but tricks of the mind, attitudes, self-induced fantasies; and let us put them from us.

Clement of Rome (30-100 A.D.)

Believers carry the image of God imprinted on them by Jesus Christ ... anything else is counterfeit

Everything must come to an end one day, and that leaves us with two alternatives: life or death. Each one of us must choose, and each one of us will receive his appointed end.

    Look at it this way. There are two different sets of coins in circulation, one the currency of God's Kingdom, the other of the world's. Each has its own distinctive markings. Unbelievers carry the image of the world. Believers carry the image of God the Father, imprinted on them by Jesus Christ. They coexist for the present, but only one is the coinage of heaven. Those who share in Christ's death receive his life, and bear the newly minted image of God. They alone are the genuine currency, valid and infinitely valuable. Anything else is counterfeit.

Ignatius of Antioch (c.35-c.107 A.D.)

Be clear in your own mind about what you will and will not do. He who hesitates is lost!

Never exaggerate your own importance. Be modest about your achievements, and in any case do not claim the credit for them. Think in a kindly way about your neighbors, without any suspicion of malice or ill will. And do not presume on God's mercy: he has no favorites, not even you!

Keep clear of every kind of sexual sin—whether it be casual promiscuity, or unfaithfulness in marriage, or some kind of sexual perversion. All are equally destructive. All lead us away from God.

When you are in the company of unbelievers, be careful how you use the word of God. Do not cheapen it by introducing it at an inappropriate moment, when it may lead to ridicule or blasphemy.

It may be that sometimes you will need to correct someone who is in the wrong. If so, be scrupulously fair, keep calm and controlled, and do not allow yourself to be resentful or arrogant towards the person involved.

Be clear in your own mind about what you will and will not do. He who hesitates is lost!

God's name is holy—do not cheapen it. Life is precious—do not cheapen that, either—whether it be the life of the unborn child, or of a fully formed man or woman. God's gifts, like his name, should be reverenced.

Epistle of Barnabas (c. 120 A.D.)

Shallow faith and shallow attitudes undermine the work of Christ in us

Imagine what it would be like if the Lord treated us in the way we treat others! It would be unbearable. We take his goodness for granted, whereas in fact we should learn from it how to behave as Christians.

Our lives should, in fact, be bursting with enthusiasm. Unfortunately, only too often we look like bread made with stale yeast—heavy, stodgy. In fact, Jesus Christ is the new yeast in our lives. It is he who infuses us with fresh lightness and flavor.

Or let's use an even more down-to-earth illustration. You can tell if meat is good by its smell. If it's been properly salted and cured it smells good. If it's been inadequately salted, or the salt has lost its properties, then it smells horrible! We are to be salted with Christ, so that we smell sweet and attractive to those around us. If we are not salted by him, then we shall have the smell of spiritual decay about us. Shallow faith and shallow attitudes undermine the work of Christ in us.

So, hold unshakably to the heart of our faith, which is Jesus Christ our hope, born, crucified and risen during the time when Pontius Pilate was governor. Let nothing turn you aside from that hope.

Ignatius of Antioch (c. 35-c.107 A.D.)

There are no short cuts to a crop of good, mature fruit

Think of a tree, when you are tempted to feel that God's promises are delayed, or begin to doubt that the Lord will come again. "We heard these promises in our fathers' time," people say, "and now we have grown old, and still these prophecies have not been fulfilled."

Think of a tree, because the process of growth there is also slow, but yet inevitable. The foliage falls after the harvest but then in the Spring a bud appears, and from the bud come leaves, and later flowers. These in turn lead on to young, unripe grapes, and finally the full cluster. It does not take very long, it is true, but the whole process must take place. No stage can be left out. There are no short cuts to a crop of good, mature fruit.

Neither can God's purposes be hurried. No stage can be left out. The whole process must take place. But let us be in no doubt that his promises will be fulfilled. "He will surely come quickly, he will not delay . . . the Lord, the Holy One you wait for, will suddenly come to his temple." So—be ready!

Clement of Rome (30-100 A.D.)

Everything God has made is in his hands

Do not give in to grief or despair when someone very dear to you dies. After all, death is a rest, an end to the troubles, anxieties and care of life. Instead of despairing, stop and think. Reflect that this is the end of every life. Become more kind and thoughtful. Adopt a more reverent attitude towards God. Turn from sin and begin a new and more satisfying style of life.

After all, Christians differ from unbelievers in this estimate of things. The unbeliever sees the great expanse of the sky and searches it for clues about his existence—he looks for God among the stars. Equally, he treats the earth as though it were his master, the provider of everything he values. Christians see the sky and praise him who set the stars in space. We look at the created earth, and feel at home in the Creator's hands. For us, the skies and the land are not gods, but the work of God. Everything he has made is in his hands.

John Chrysostom (347-407 A.D.)

One day... you will stand before your judge

My brothers, let's have some humility. Let's forget all this self-promotion and ego-boosting, and all the petty squabbling about status, and instead start doing what the Bible commands: "The wise man shouldn't boast of his wisdom, nor the strong man of his strength, nor the rich man of his wealth. If we must boast, let's boast of what the Lord has done."

And Jesus had something to say about this, too. "Be merciful," he advised, "and then people will have mercy on you. Forgive, and then others will forgive you. Treat others with kindness, and they will treat you kindly as well. But if you constantly assume the role of critic, judging and condemning others, beware. One day the roles will change. You will stand before your judge, and he will condemn you."

We should listen to these words, and let them strengthen our determination to pursue humility of mind. After all, God says, "Who wins my approval? The person who is gentle, calm ... and trembles at my words."

Clement of Rome (30-100 A.D.)

It is a mark of spiritual maturity to know when to be silent

The Christian life begins and ends with just two qualities: faith, which is the beginning, and love, which is the goal. And they are attributes of God himself. All that makes for holiness flows from them, for no one who wholly believes will commit sin, and no one who wholly loves can feel hatred.

We recognize a tree by its fruit, and we ought to be able to recognize a Christian by his actions. The fruit of faith should be evident in our lives, for being a Christian is more than a matter of making sound *professions* of faith. It should reveal itself in practical and visible ways.

Indeed, it is better to keep quiet about our beliefs, and live them out, than to talk eloquently about what we believe but fail to live by it. Of course, it is very commendable to teach the Christian faith to others, but only if the instructor is practicing what he preaches.

After all, the perfect Teacher, whose words carried miraculous power, also spoke eloquently by his silences. It's very revealing to see how often Jesus said nothing, but by his behavior or his attitude—or simply by the force of his own personality—achieved the perfect result. That is a mark of spiritual maturity—to know when to speak, but also when to be silent.

If we are feeling desperate, you save us from our own sense of failure

> Teach us, Holy Father...
>> to hope in your name, from whom everything
>> that exists has come.
> Open our inward eyes
>> to recognize you, although you are
>> the highest in high heaven, and the holy one
>> among all the ranks of the holy.
> You, Lord God,
>> bring down the proud and outwit the cunning;
>> promote the humble, and make the arrogant fall;
>> hold in your hand every issue of life—
>> whether we are to be rich or poor, whether
>> we are to live or die;
>> see every spirit, good or evil,
>> and the inner thoughts and intentions
>> of every person.
> If we are in danger, you come to our aid.
> If we are feeling desperate, you save us from
>> our own sense of failure.
> If events in the world overshadow us, we remember
>> that you are the creator and overseer
>> of every living being.

Clement of Rome (30-100 A.D.)

Let the people know that you alone are God, that Jesus Christ is your Son, and that we are your children

By you, Lord,
human life comes into existence,
and spiritual life comes to those who love you
through your Son Jesus Christ.
And by him we have learned the truth
and our lives have been pointed
toward holiness and self-respect.
Grant, Lord,
your help and protection:
for those afflicted, deliverance;
for those deprived of their rights, pity;
for those fallen into sin, rescue;
for those who know they need you, a sight
of yourself;
for those who are ill, healing;
for those who are wandering, a safe journey home.
Let all the people of the world know that you alone are God, that Jesus Christ is your son, and that we are your children.

e as though he had never been born, or died, or risen?

If we are still slaves to the Jewish religious law, it shows that we have failed to receive the grace of Jesus Christ. Why, even the Jewish prophets, who foretold his coming, were inspired by Christ—that is why they were persecuted!

So you can look around you today in the church and see how those who formerly followed the Jewish religion have now realized this new hope and believe, with us, in one God who has revealed himself in his Son Jesus Christ, his own Word uttered out of the silence of eternity. They have been released from slavery to the law. They have given up keeping the sabbath and now, instead, recognize the Lord's Day, that day when life first broke through in the resurrection of Jesus, who had died for us. That death, whatever some of our detractors say, is the heart of the mystery which we believe and by which we are saved.

So how can we fall back into a kind of religion that takes no account of the fact that Christ has come? How can we live as though he had never been born, or died, or risen? The prophets of old looked forward eagerly to what we have been privileged to experience. (That is why he visited them and raised them from the dead[1].) We must not take this privilege lightly.

[1]*See 1 Peter 3:19,20*

Ignatius of Antioch (c.35-c.107 A.D.)

Our money can feed the hungry and clothe the poor

Don't despise possessions. And don't despise profits, either. After all, possessions are "possessed" by us: they are our servants, not our masters. And profits are "profitable," or they should be.

Wealth is at our disposal, an instrument which can be used well or foolishly. How it is used doesn't depend on the instrument, but on the person who is using it. If we use it well, it is a valuable servant—a servant which can do good things for us, and for those who depend on us. If we use it badly, it is an unhelpful servant—a servant which causes us and our friends endless harm. We shouldn't blame what is blameless. Wealth in itself is neither good nor evil.

So where does the blame lie for all the evil done in the name of money and possessions? Not in the things themselves: they are harmlessly neutral. The evil is in the mind of man himself—man who by the free will and moral independence God has given him manages what he owns. Human desires express themselves through a man's possessions—desire to impress others, perhaps, or competitive instincts, which drive him always to rival his affluent neighbor. But those desires can also be noble ones, and express themselves in noble ways. Our money can feed the hungry and clothe the poor.

Clement of Alexandria (155-220 A.D.)

The great cannot exist without the small, nor the small without the great

There is a battle to be fought, my friends, so let's get on with it. But let's remember who is directing operations.

We are all familiar with the way the Imperial Army operates in the field, each man giving instant and efficient obedience to his officer's orders. And this is true right through the army—from the lowliest trooper to the general himself, each man obeys the orders of the Emperor which come to him through his immediate superior.

There is no other way to run an army. The Emperor himself cannot exist without the obedience of all those men who make up his military. Nor can they survive without the protection and guidance of the Emperor. The great cannot exist without the small, nor the small without the great.

This is true of every organism, including the Church of Christ. It is this mutual dependence, this unity of differing elements, which ensures the health of the whole organism. The body, for instance, needs both the head and the feet. The feet are useless without a head to guide them, but the head cannot move the body without the feet. Even our smallest and simplest organs and limbs are necessary and valuable. Every part works together in common obedience, if the body is to function properly.

Clement of Rome (30-100 A.D.)

Jesus came to invite men, not to drive them to repentance

When a great king sends an emissary to a rebellious people, you expect a mission of ruthless power and terror. But when God sent his Son to us rebels, he sent him in gentleness and humility, although he was a King sending a son who was also a King.

He sent Jesus as God, but he also sent him as a Man to men. He sent him on an errand of mercy, of persuasion, not of *force*. Force is foreign to the nature of God. Jesus came to invite men, not to drive them to repentance. And God's motive in sending him was love, not judgment . . . though one day he *will* send him in judgment, and "who will abide the day of his coming?"

How do we know that he came, the Son of God, the Son of Man? We know as we see the results of his coming—as we see his followers refuse to deny him, even though they are flung to wild beasts or tortured; as we see their numbers increase as persecution increases; as we see that nothing can conquer their faith in the Lord. Such things are not the work of mortal man. They are evidence of the power of God. They are the proofs of Christ's presence.

Epistle to Diognetus (c. 150 A.D.)

I will do anything... if it will contribute to peace among Christ's flock

Suppose there is friction and bad feeling in your church—what should you do, especially if you are involved in the arguments and divisions yourself?

Further, let's suppose that you are in the right, that the trouble is not your fault, and that you are a mature and compassionate person.

In that case, I suggest that you should say to the elders and members of the church: "If I am in any way the cause of this trouble, even if unwittingly, or if my presence will in any way serve to perpetuate it, I will move to another congregation, however inconvenient or humiliating an experience that might be. I will go away anywhere you wish, and do anything the congregation says—anything, if it will contribute to peace among Christ's flock and its pastors."

Anyone who adopts this attitude will deserve a high reputation among Christians, and God's approval. And he will be sure of a welcome by another congregation, for "the earth is the Lord's, and everything in it."

Clement of Rome (30-100 A.D.)

If we imitate Christ, we won't go wrong

What should we do about those around us who are not believers? Certainly we should pray for them, not just occasionally or as a matter of routine but all the time, in the hope that they may have a change of heart and so find their way to God.

But we should also give them every opportunity to learn the truth of Christ from us, not so much, perhaps, by our preaching it to them in so many words, but by the way we behave towards them. Our attitude should reflect the attitude of Christ.

So, when they are hostile, meet them with gentleness. When they make angry accusations, respond with calm words. When they abuse you, pray for them.

At the same time, don't compromise your beliefs or water them down to make them acceptable. It is possible to stand firm against violence and error while remaining perfectly calm and gentle. Don't be trapped into playing their game with them!

Let's show them that we regard them as our brothers, children of the same Creator, and simply want them to become also our brothers in Christ, sons of the same Father. Our attitude should be that of the Lord Jesus. If we imitate him, we won't go wrong.

Ignatius of Antioch (c.35-c.107 A.D.)

They have everything they want and yet have few possessions

Like everyone else, Christians have physical bodies, of course, but their lives aren't dominated by them. They are nationals of various states but citizens of heaven. They keep the law, but in their own lives go far beyond it.

Despite all this, they aren't very popular! They set themselves to love everyone, even their enemies, yet they are persecuted more than any other people on earth. They are condemned by people who know nothing about them. They are the great proclaimers of life, so everyone sets out to kill them. They believe in a God who makes men rich, and yet often they are themselves penniless. They have everything they want, and yet have few possessions. Everybody tries to discredit them, but the result is always the same—they are shown up in their true colors, and honored instead of disgraced.

Epistle to Diognetus (c. 150 A.D.)

What sense is there in trying to run away from the will of God?

God's generosity is a wonderful thing, freely offered. But if we abuse it, turning on one another and destroying the fellowship, that very generosity may condemn us. There is no sin greater than the sin against love.

The Spirit of the Lord is like a beam of light scanning the inner recesses of our being. Let's remember this, then. Not a single thought, not a single twisted motive, escapes his notice. He probes everything, he sees everything, and he is near us all the time.

So what sense is there in trying to run away from the will of God? Or, even worse, to oppose him? Better by far to set ourselves to oppose his enemies, to reject their arrogance, to turn a deaf ear to their attempts to divide the church in their own selfish interests.

Let's realize that it is the humble spirit that really wins, and the proud one that always loses in the end. God exalts the humble, and humbles the proud. For he is the one who examines our thoughts and intentions. His is the breath that keeps us alive, and he, in his own good time, will take it away. What can we do but reverence him?

Clement of Rome (30-100 A.D.)

re laid out on the altar under the scrutiny of God

All kinds of trouble flow from the love of money. Yet we are well aware that "we brought nothing into the world, and we can carry nothing out". Some day we shall live without money, so we should prepare ourselves now by accepting the discipline of putting God's commandments first, and ensuring that integrity is our watchword whenever money is concerned.

When the elders have done that, we shall be in a position to advise the women in the congregation about their manner of life. They should be taught Christian attitudes of love and loyalty. Affectionate and true to their husbands, they should be careful about their relationships with other men. Ideally, they should be friendly and warm in an impartial way with everyone, rather than having special men friends, and they should, of course, avoid any suggestion of impurity.

The widows in the congregation need special help if they are to witness to their faith. They have a particular calling to intercessory prayer for the other members of the church, but this ministry is spoiled if they also spend time spreading gossip and spiteful rumors, stirring up trouble by making unfounded allegations, or acquiring money.

They should realize that they are supported by the sacrificial gifts of others. In that sense, their lives are laid out on the altar, under the scrutiny of God, from whom no secrets can be hidden.

Polycarp of Smyrna (c. 69-155 A.D.)

The spirit that is in man speaks in various languages, but what it says is always the same

The soul is not the exclusive possession of so-called "civilized" races. Man is one and the same everywhere, and so is the soul. The spirit that is in man speaks in various languages, but what it says is always the same.

Its message is that God is everywhere, and so is his goodness; that the devil and his curse are also everywhere; that God's judgment applies everywhere, and that everywhere man is aware of it, however reluctantly. The witness of the soul is universal.

This means that the soul is also under that divine judgment, and it is guilty of evil, even while it witnesses to the truth. You see, it points to God, but does not seek him. It recognizes that demons are evil, but casually accepts their influence. It knows that there is a hell, but takes no precautions to avoid it. It is made to be a temple for Christ, but in fact excludes him.

The soul makes man a rational being. It separates him from the animals. It is the seat of sense and intellectual knowledge. But in spiritual things it can be an unreliable witness.

Tertullian (c. 160-c. 220 A.D.)

God has acted: Jesus Christ has come... a new age has dawned

I am now the servant of the Cross—that same Cross which repels and appalls the unbeliever, but which means life and health to us. "Where is your wise man now, and where is your clever deba-ter?" Where are the sophisticated words of our "intellectuals?" God has acted: Jesus Christ has come, conceived by Mary of David's ancestry and of the Holy Spirit, born, baptized, suffering, and victorious.

Until these days, evil forces have dominated the world—magic, evil spirits, superstition. But the coming of Jesus took them by surprise. Even the "prince of this world" was totally un-aware of what was happening in Mary's womb. He did not realize the deep meaning of the birth of Jesus, nor of his crucifixion. God hoodwinked the powers of evil, outwitted them, and de-feated them by his own, silent wisdom, by these three mysterious cries from the heart of the universe.

How was the secret of the coming of Jesus announced to the world? A star shone, more brilliant than the rest. It baffled the experts—the men of magic, the seers. They had no explanation for its sudden appearance.

And with that star a new age dawned, for the old powers of magic and sorcery were broken, and superstition received its death-blow. The age-old empire of evil crumbled, for God was now appearing in human form to bring in a new age, a new king-dom, and life that never ends.

Ignatius of Antioch (c. 35-c. 107 A.D.)

The real test always lies in our attitudes

Possessions are external things, but our desires are within us. It is quite useless to try to reform the external objects if we have not first resolved the internal motivation. We may give all our money away, but what use is that if the longing for it still burns inside us? Poor people can covet. Poor people can envy. And poor people can misuse the little money they have. Getting rid of our material possessions will do nothing, in itself, to create in us a right attitude towards them.

Yes, the real test always lies in our *attitudes*. We can enjoy our possessions, seeing them as God's generous gifts, and using them as much for others as for ourselves. We can possess them without allowing them to possess us.

Only then can we be quite sure that if, in God's will, we are ever deprived of them, we may accept their loss as contentedly as we did their superabundance.

Clement of Alexandria (155-220 A.D.)

We have his command to put all our energy and enthusiasm into our work

There's nothing wrong with work. Even the Lord and Architect of the universe not only works, but enjoys working. For his own satisfaction and pleasure he created the skies and set the stars in order. He divided the dry land from the waters and marked out their boundaries. He gave life to the animals that live on that land, as well as to the creatures who live in the waters. And then, to complete his labors, he formed man, in his own likeness. His works of creation were ended.

Only then did he pause, satisfied, to give them his blessing.

So if God himself could find joy and satisfaction in his work—work well done, work completed—so may we. We already have his *command* to put all our energy and enthusiasm into our work, doing it "heartily, as for the Lord." Now let us add his *example*, and spare no effort to obey his will for us.

Clement of Rome (30-100 A.D.)

No one who does his work "before the Lord" will miss his reward

You needn't be ashamed of the money you earn, provided you *earn* it. But if you don't—if you're a half-hearted, unreliable employee—then, of course, you'll probably be embarrassed every time you meet your boss.

For Christians, the "boss" is God. That is why we should work with all our hearts and souls. We are answerable to the Lord for the quality of our work, and it is simply impossible to avoid meeting him: "Look," says Scripture, "the Lord is approaching, bringing rewards, to pay each man as his work deserves."

So he tells us never to be lazy or inefficient in any piece of work. No one who does his work "before the Lord" will miss his reward. Think of the angels, that vast company of heaven, spending every moment in his service, waiting instantly to obey each of his commands! "Ten thousand times ten thousand stand before him and thousands of thousands serve him, crying, 'Holy holy, holy, Lord of hosts: all creation is full of his glory.' "

That should be a picture for us of our work: our daily work, done for his glory; and our work of praise and witness in the church, gathered together in perfect unity to do his will.

Clement of Rome (30-100 A.D.)

In the arena of the daily routine there are heroes, and crowns await them

"Crowns of glory" are promised to Christians who are faithful "unto *death*;" but Christian *life* also has its crowns. Victories in other kinds of conflict are also honored, and the victors crowned.

There is a victor's palm for the Christian who overcomes sexual temptation. There is a crown of patience for those who resist anger and revenge. There is honor for those who reject the lure of money.

The shout of triumph will greet those who suffer the world's opposition, but continue to trust in God; those who accept success and prosperity with modesty and humility; those who care for the poor and hungry; those who genuinely love their fellowmen, without jealousy or envy.

In the arena of the daily routine there are heroes as honorable and as brave as the martyrs of the faith, and the palms and the crowns await them as well.

Cyprian (200-258 A.D.)

No man is prepared to die for a shadow

If you come across somebody who says that Jesus Christ never lived, or that he's just an idea, or a concept, or a myth—shut your ears to him.

Jesus Christ was born into a human family, a descendant of David. His mother was Mary. He was persecuted and crucified under Pontius Pilate, a fact testified to us by some who are now in heaven, and some who are still alive on earth. How can this be a phantom, or an illusion, or a myth? These are facts of history!

It is also a fact that he rose from the dead (or rather, that his Father raised him up). And that is the most important "fact" of all, because his promise is that the Father will also raise us up, if we believe in him. So if Christ Jesus is not alive, neither shall we be. There is nothing left for us to hope for if he is just an idea or a fantasy.

In any case, if he only *appeared* to live, and only *appeared* to die, and only *appeared* to rise from the dead—why should I be in chains for this "myth?" Why should I die to support an illusion? I am prepared to die for him, the true and real Son of God. But no man is prepared to die for a shadow.

Ignatius of Antioch (c. 35-c. 107 A.D.)

The brighter your reputation, the harder it is to be humble

Loving one another, and putting the welfare of others before our own, is the open door to life: "Open for me the gate of righteousness, that I may go in and praise the Lord; the righteous shall come in by it." And this *is* the gate of righteousness and the gate of Christ, the door to life, the entrance into a place of blessing. That way is open only to those who pursue holiness and integrity, and avoid creating strife.

By all means master the great doctrines of the Christian faith, and defend them. By all means utter the secrets of God's revelation, evaluating and interpreting what you hear from the lips of others.

But the brighter your reputation in the Church and the more the ordinary people look up to you—the harder it will be for you to be humble. It is at that moment, more than any other, that a person should pray for humility, and set his ambition firmly on serving and building up the people of God, rather than his own reputation.

Clement of Rome (30-100 A.D.)

Only when I get to the light will I truly be a man

All the way from Syria to Rome I have been chained to a detachment of soldiers who have behaved like animals towards me. I tried giving them money, but the more I gave them the more roughly they treated me. Quite honestly, they are like a pack of leopards, enjoying their role as hunters, with me as their prey.

Well, that has some advantages. I may as well get used to "leopards" now—it will be lions, and real ones at that, when I get to Rome. So I can make some progress towards preparing myself spiritually and mentally for what lies ahead.

All I pray is that when the moment comes the lions will be quick about it. Some Christians have suffered torments because the animals have toyed with them. If my lions are like that, I shall antagonize them!

Forgive me for writing like this, but I do know what is best for me. No power, human or spiritual, must hinder my coming to Jesus Christ. So whether the way be fire, or crucifixion, or wild beasts in the arena, or the mangling of my whole body, I can bear it, provided I am assured it is the way to him.

And it is! All the riches and power in the world cannot compare with that. So far as I am concerned, to die in Jesus Christ is better than to be king of the whole wide world! Do not try to tempt me to stay here by offering me the world and its attractions. Just let me make my way upward to that pure and undiluted light. For only when I get there will I truly be a *man*.

Ignatius of Antioch (c. 35-c. 107 A.D.)

I thank you today for the privilege of sharing the cup of suffering which Christ drank

Lord God almighty, Father of your dear and blessed Son Jesus Christ, through whom we have been granted to know you; You are God over all: over angels and other spiritual powers, over the whole created universe, and over those good people from every age who live in your presence.

I thank you today for the privilege of being counted among those who have witnessed to you with their lives; of sharing the cup of suffering which Christ drank; and of rising again to life everlasting with him, in body and soul, and in the immortality of the Holy Spirit.

May I be received today into your presence, a costly sacrifice and so an acceptable one. This is all part of your plan and purpose, and you are now bringing it to pass. For you are the God of truth, and in you is no falsehood at all.

For this, and for all the other things you have done for me, I bless and glorify you, through our eternal high Priest in heaven, your dear Son, Jesus Christ, who shares with you and the Holy Spirit glory for ever. Amen.

Polycarp of Smyrna (c. 69-155 A.D.)

Jesus Christ, the High Priest, is our Protector on earth and the appointed way to heaven

God's gifts are marvelous, aren't they? Some of them we know and enjoy already: the experience of life that knows no death; the splendor of his sheer goodness; the truth that is honest and complete; faith that gives assurance and confidence in God; a purity that is infinitely better than self-indulgence.

But there are other gifts of God which by their very nature we cannot know yet. They can only be revealed by the Creator and Father of eternity, and only he knows how magnificent they are. But if they are better than the gifts we know already, how wonderful, how utterly desirable they must be!

For such gifts it is worth waiting patiently. But it is also worth straining every nerve to achieve them, by fixing our minds on the Giver, by seeking to discover his will for us and then doing it; by renouncing deceit and pursuing truth. And—most of all—by coming to Jesus Christ, the High Priest who is the appointed way to heaven and our Protector on earth. Through him alone can our eyes look up to the highest heaven, even to the face of God. Through him alone the Father allows us to taste those wonderful joys of eternity, all of which are "in him."

Clement of Rome (30-100 A.D.)

The body God first created by his art will one day be re-made by God's power

How can those who believe in God as the Creator doubt his ability to raise the dead?

Look at it this way. In the beginning God took the dust of the earth and from it created man. Just think what was involved in that act of creation—to make a living, rational creature, with bones, muscles, veins and all the other organs, out of a handful of dust!

Surely that act of creation was far harder, far more incredible, than the re-creation of the same being after it has returned to dust again?

If God could give personal existence, at a moment of his own choice, to someone who a moment before did not exist at all, surely he can restore to that same person the life he originally gave him, if he so wishes?

In fact, the body God first created by his art—our own mortal flesh—will one day be found capable of being re-made by God's power. What will be restored to life will not be something other than that which died, but its former physical life will be transformed by the Spirit of God into spiritual life for ever.

Irenaeus (c. 130-c. 202 A.D.)

Those who hold fast to the faith will be saved by the One who bore the curse of sin for us

Guard your way of life. Never let your lamps go out or be caught unprepared. Be ready, because you simply do not know the moment of the Lord's return.

Come together often, to strengthen each other spiritually, because all your past faithfulness will be no help at that moment, unless you have sustained your faith. For in those last days false prophets and deceivers will be everywhere, leading the flock away. Some sheep will turn into wolves and love will turn to hate, persecution and betrayal.

At that point the great Deceiver will appear, pretending to be a son of God and performing miracles and wonders. The whole world will fall into his hands, and evil will dominate as it has never done before. All the human race will be put on trial, as it were—a trial by fire. Many will fail the test and perish. But those who hold fast to the faith will be saved by the One who bore the curse of sin for us.

And then the signs of truth will appear—the opening skies, the trumpet's blast, the resurrection of the dead. The Lord will come, and all his holy ones with him—and every eye shall see him riding on the clouds of heaven!

Didache (c. 80 A.D.)

...ment, friends of ours are at the side of the Lord in heaven

It's a wonderful thought that at this moment friends of ours, people we have known and loved, are at the side of the Lord in heaven, sharing his joy as once they shared his pains. Their hearts were never wedded to this world and its values, but were focused on him who died for us, and was raised from the dead for us by God.

So copy them, as they copied Christ. Hold the faith firmly, join together to defend the truth, and love one another as brothers. Indeed, make a habit of giving way to one another, not regarding any one as inferior or beneath your attention. In that way you will have the spirit of Christ, who never treated any person with anything less than courtesy and love, however poor, or sinful, or outcast they were.

Polycarp of Smyrna (c. 69-155 A.D.)

When I put off the old, that I had longed to lose, then I put on the new, the Lord Christ, whom I had longed to find

It was depressing even to think of it. "How long?" I asked the Lord, "How long will you be angry with me? For ever? Can't you forget my sins?"

You see, even if *he* forgot, I couldn't; and I couldn't believe he forgot, either. I felt trapped still by my past failures. So I cried to him: "Why not *now*, Lord—why not, at this very moment, put an end to this uncleanness?"

And the moment I said it, he answered. I heard a voice, a far-away voice like a child calling from a distant house, repeating over and over again, "Pick up the book and read. Pick up the book and read."

So I picked up the book. It was the letters of the apostle Paul. I opened it, and I read silently the first words on which my eyes fell: "Not parties, not getting drunk, not promiscuity, not quarrelling and envy—put off all those. But put on the Lord Christ, and stop encouraging your lower nature."

I needed to read no more, for instantly—by the end of the sentence—a clear, bright light shone into my heart, driving out the darkness of my doubts. It seemed so straightforward. When I put off the old, that I had longed to lose, then I put on the new, the Lord Christ, whom I had longed to find.

Augustine of Hippo (354-430 A.D.)

A heart that glorifies its Creator releases a sweet perfume for the Lord

Of one thing there cannot be any doubt. The Lord has made it abundantly clear, through his prophets, that he has not the smallest need of sacrifices, burnt offerings and oblations. His exact words are: "What do I care about all these sacrifices of yours? says the Lord. I have had enough of them. I do not want the fat of lambs, nor the blood of bulls and goats, nor your presence here before me. Do not enter my courts; it is useless to offer me gifts of fine flour. I detest incense, and I cannot stand all these new moons, festivals and sabbaths."

In Jesus Christ, God swept all these things away. He intended a new order, which did not impose laws and rituals on its followers, and whose sacrificial offering is not made by human hands.

So how are we to approach him, if not with gifts, sacrifices and offerings? He gives us the answer himself: "The sacrifice of which the Lord approves is a contrite heart." And again: "A heart that glorifies its Creator releases a sweet perfume for the Lord."[1] It is to us that he is speaking here, in the hope that we should follow the right way to him, the way of humility, contrition and love for our neighbor. "None of you is to tolerate an evil thought in his heart against a neighbor, nor any approval of broken promises."

[1] *The source of this quotation is lost.*

Epistle of Barnabas (c. 120 A.D.)

The Holy Spirit cannot be mistaken, because he comes from God, and God is infallible

Now of course I am not infallible! Like everyone else, I can be mistaken. But the Holy Spirit can't be deceived or mistaken, because he comes from God, and God *is* infallible.

Let me give you an example. When I visited your church at Philadelphia there was a faction in the church that was undermining the authority of the church's leadership and questioning their decisions. *Now God is my witness that I knew nothing about this at all.* No one had told me about it, and no rumor of it had reached my ears.

So when I stood up to prophesy, and shouted in a loud voice, "Give more respect to your bishop, your elders and your deacons!" it was the Holy Spirit in me who was speaking. Although I know some of you think I had been told in advance of the divisions at Philadelphia, and spoke from knowledge, the absolute truth is that this was the voice of God alone.

So remember and obey the other things I said as well: "Keep your bodies as temples of God. Love unity. Shun divisions. Follow Jesus Christ, as he followed his Father."

Ignatius of Antioch (c. 35-c. 107 A.D.)

Knowledge leads to life, and life leads to knowledge

Those who love God truly become another garden of Eden, a new paradise, and in their hearts every kind of fruit springs up. For in that garden are planted again the Tree of Knowledge and the Tree of Life. You see, it was not the Tree of Knowledge as such that caused death to our first parents in Eden, but their disobedience.

The Bible says, "In the beginning God planted in the midst of the garden the tree of knowledge and the tree of life". This indicates that the way to life is through knowledge. It was not wrong of Adam and Eve to want knowledge, but it was a deadly sin to disobey God and acquire that knowledge improperly. That is why they were expelled from the garden and lost everything.

In fact, there can be no life without knowledge, and there can be no reliable knowledge without life, which is why the two trees were planted side by side. Knowledge without life's love is just empty wind, for the man who claims to know, but is without the life-giving principles of love, in fact knows nothing. Knowledge leads to life, and life—spiritual life—leads to knowledge. It is the devil's work to try and keep the two apart.

Epistle to Diognetus (c. 150 A.D.)

Your heart will be the Garden of Eden: knowledge and life will abound there

Set your heart on life with God, and you may confidently expect to sow in hope and gather in a rich harvest of fruit. Your heart will indeed be like the garden of Eden, and by planting the Word of God in this fertile soil, knowledge and life will abound there.

How pleasant this garden will be! Tending the trees, and gathering the fruit, your harvest will be pleasing to God—and it will be one which that serpent, the devil, will not be able to spoil.

In that garden, Eve cannot be seduced to disobedience. Knowledge and life flow into it from the Virgin's Son, and from it flows salvation for those around. Here the evangelist will find his message fresh and new, worship is lifted onto a higher plane, the Word brings joy and assurance to the believers, and God is glorified.

Knowledge and life—keep them together, and God will be glorified!

Epistle to Diognetus (c. 150 A.D.)

There is only one Healer, from this or any wound, physical or spiritual

It is sadly possible to bear the Name of Christ and yet live a life totally unworthy of God. And in some cases those who behave like this do it deliberately. They want to be known as Christians so as to infiltrate your ranks and cause as much trouble for you as they can. Like mad dogs, their bite is sudden and unexpected, but once you are bitten, healing is a slow and painful matter— and not all recover.

In fact, there is only one Healer, from this or any other wound, physical or spiritual. He is the One who had no beginning, and yet was born on earth; who is God, and yet is also man; who won true life through dying; who is the Son of Mary and also the Son of God; who suffered once, but suffers no more: Jesus Christ, our Lord.

Ignatius of Antioch (c. 35-c. 107 A.D.)

To cut oneself off from the Body of Christ, where the light shines, is to choose darkness

Although the Church of Jesus Christ is found in many different places, she is one Church, not many. After all, there are many rays of sunlight, but only one sun. A tree has many boughs, each slightly different from the others, but all drawing their strength from one source. Many streams may flow down a hill-side, but they all originate from the same spring. In exactly the same way each local congregation belongs to the one Church.

If you put a solid object across a ray of the sun it disappears, cut off from its source of light. If you break a branch off a tree, it dies and can never bud again. And if you dam up a stream, the course will soon dry up.

The Church offers the light of Christ to the world, flooding out from him who is the source of all light. Cut off that light, and the darkness is total. To cut oneself off from the Body of Christ, where the light shines, is to choose darkness.

The Church stretches out her branches all over the earth, offering shelter and refreshment to the weary. And she also pours out the living water, which we can drink and never thirst again.

At all costs, let's make sure that we are not guilty, by our divisions, of cutting off from men and women that light, that shelter and that water of life.

Cyprian (200-258 A.D.)

He still cares for them; so must we

I am worried about those who have lapsed. Once they followed Christ, but they have fallen away, perhaps into serious sin, or perhaps they have just become slack and careless.

Remember that they are brothers. They have not forfeited their privileges as children of God. He still cares for them; so must we.

If any of them falls ill, act at once. Don't wait for special instructions from me. Go to them, urge them to repent and confess their sins, and then assure them that should they die they will go to the Lord in peace.

With regard to the other backsliders, keep in touch with them. Encourage them not to abandon their belief in the Lord's mercy towards those who repent. Assure them that if they humbly and sincerely confess their sins, and turn back to God, he will receive them and give them his strength and support to change their way of life. His grace is as freely available to them as it is to the rest of us.

Be equally concerned about the young people, and the new converts. Keep an eye on them. Difficulties can arise very quickly. But God's grace is speedy, too, and he never denies his mercy to those who seek it.

Cyprian (200-258 A.D.)

What will our future rewards be if our present joys are so many and so wonderful?

I have wrapped up in my mind a kind of gift package of blessings! If I decided to take them singly, to unwrap each one and examine it, with all the varied details of God's goodness contained within it, how long it would take!

What then will our future rewards be, if our present joys are so many and so wonderful? What blessings in that life of heaven's happiness will he provide for those for whom he willed that his only-begotten Son should endure such sufferings, even death? Surely that is why the Apostle promises to us this joy: "God did not spare his own Son, but gave him up on behalf of us all. Then is it not certain that with this gift he will give us all he has to give?"

When this promise is fulfilled, what kind of beings shall we be? What blessings will we receive in that kingdom, seeing that in Christ's death for us we have already received such a pledge? What will man's spirit be like when it is free from any imperfection, when there are no evil tendencies for him to be tempted by, or to yield to, or to fight against—however praiseworthy such a struggle may be!

How complete, and how sure will be our knowledge of all things, a knowledge without error, involving no striving on our part. For there we shall drink of God's Wisdom at its very source.

Augustine of Hippo (354-430 A.D.)

For those who have chosen to major in holiness, there is a special training in the Word

It is the task of the Word of God to be our guardian, our moral and spiritual instructor. He teaches us to love freedom, to love our fellow man, to love and admire what is excellent, rather than merely what is effective or adequate. The Word will not permit us to get away with carelessness or mediocrity.

We all accept that there is special training for philosophers, for teachers, for athletes. Equally, for those who have chosen to major in holiness, there is a special training in the Word. It involves, as does any serious training, almost every detail of life: walking, eating, resting, working, every part is disciplined and every part contributes to the goal of spiritual health and beauty.

Mind you, this training (unlike some of the others) does not put people under emotional or physical strain and tension. It is not a matter of driving oneself to the limit so much as allowing the Word to show us our weaknesses and moral flaws, and then bringing us the Savior's own remedies, precisely gauged to meet every specific need.

Clement of Alexandria (155-220 A.D.)

We were nothing when we came into the world . . . everything we have comes from him

Just as in our physical bodies every part contributes something important to the whole, so it is with our corporate body in Christ, the Church. Each of us should give way to his neighbor, according to the spiritual gifts the Lord has given him. The strong should not overlook the problems of their weaker brethren, and the weak should recognize the gifts of the strong. Wealthy Christians should share their riches with the poorer members; and those who benefit from their generosity should thank God for it.

But it goes further than that. If a man has a gift of wisdom, let him express it not just in words but by good deeds, noting the needs of those around him. If someone else has the gift of modesty, let him leave others to say how modest he is—his claim is somewhat contradicted if he draws attention to it himself! If another Christian has achieved self-control in sexual matters, he should not boast about it. Instead, he should recognize that this too is a gift from the Lord, not some "strength" of his own.

After all, we were nothing when we came into the world, and we owned nothing, either. Everything we have, physically, spiritually and morally, comes from him and is his gift. So . . . glorify him!

Clement of Rome (30-100 A.D.)

Judgment begins and ends with holiness—it is its measure and its objective

There are three great divine principles.

The first is that faith begins and ends with hope—hope of eternal life. It is the hope of eternal life that draws us to faith, and it is faith that brings us to the hope of eternal life.

The second is that judgment begins and ends with holiness—it is its only measure and its only objective.

And the third is that holy actions are marked by love, and the joy and gladness that spring from it.

Not only that, but the Lord has sealed these promises through the Prophets, by laying open to us the past, explaining the present, and even giving us an anticipatory glimpse into the future. So, when we see things happening exactly as he has foretold them, it should enrich and deepen our respect and trust in him.

That is especially true in difficult times like these, when it almost seems the Evil One himself is in control of events. It means we must apply ourselves more than ever to a careful study of what God has done and promised, patiently and reverently reinforcing our faith as we see his Word being fulfilled. If we can hold fast the faith and seek holiness, the Lord will also give us wisdom, insight and understanding of the times.

Epistle of Barnabas (c. 120 A.D.)

Persecution served to unify our churches and bring some waverers into a more committed faith

The servants of Christ living in Vienne and Lyons in France send their Christian greetings to the brethren in Asia who share our hope and our redemption. Peace, grace and glory to you from God the Father and our Lord Jesus Christ!

This letter is to tell you of the things we have suffered recently, and of the courage of our martyrs.

It began in a small way. With official encouragement, the people—our neighbors—began to turn against us. We were first of all banned from the public baths and the market, and then from appearing in public at all. This we were able to bear. In fact, it served to unify our churches and bring some who had been waverers into a more committed faith.

The next stage was harder to bear. The people began to conduct a campaign of physical harrassment against us. We were jostled and punched if we ventured out of doors. Our possessions were stolen or damaged, and a noisy crowd gathered outside our homes, shouting insults and throwing stones at our windows.

In the end, the authorities intervened—not to protect us, as you might have imagined, but by arresting most of our leading Christians and putting them on public trial before the tribune in the market place. When they had been questioned, they were locked up in the town jail to await the governor's arrival.

The Churches of Vienne and Lyons (177 A.D.)

"Are you a Christian?" he asked him. When he said he was... the governor ordered him to be killed there and then

When the governor arrived, we were all flogged, and then brought before him. At this point, one of our young men, Vettius Epagathus, stepped forward and asked if he could speak. He was a highly respected man in the town, and an outstanding young Christian, enthusiastic and full of the Holy Spirit.

Unable to stand silently by and watch the Christians being treated so unfairly, he spoke up forcefully that we were not blasphemers or irreligious people, but honest and hard-working citizens. The governor interrupted him, "Are you a Christian?" he asked him. When Vettius said that he was, in a clear and steady voice, the governor ordered him to be killed there and then.

The sight of this brother of ours being martyred caused some of our number to waver. Most of us, though appalled at the prospect, were ready to be put to the sword. A few, however—mostly new believers or those who were uninstructed or weak in the faith—denied Christ in the hope that they would then escape execution. There were about ten whose courage failed them, but they were quickly replaced by other Christians who had previously been overlooked but were now brought in by the soldiers and locked up with us. Eventually, all the committed members of both churches were in custody.

"I am a Christian, and evil cannot find a place among us."

At this point, needing some "evidence" with which to convict us, the governor ordered that all our heathen domestic servants should be arrested. The threat of torture by the soldiers was enough to produce from among them witnesses who were ready to witness that the Christians engaged in private orgies and all kinds of sexual perversions. These accusations served to turn the general population against us, and even those who had been sympathetic towards us now joined in demanding our deaths. It was another fulfilment of our Lord's prophecy: "The time will come when those who kill you will think they are doing God a service."

All of us, from that point, were tortured every day, but the brunt of the ill-treatment was borne by three of the Christians: Sanctus, a deacon from the Vienne church; Maturus, a comparatively new convert but a brave man; and a servant-girl called Blandina.

She was incredible—a living proof of the apostle Paul's words that those who count for little in the world's eyes may gain great glory in the sight of God.

She was a woman from the lowest ranks of the community, physically unattractive and despised by most of those who knew her. Yet when her mistress, a Christian who was with us in prison, began to waver in her faith, it was Blandina who strengthened her. Seeing what a strength she was to us all, the soldiers took her away and tortured her unbelievably, until her body was mangled and covered with gaping wounds, so that they couldn't believe she was still alive.

But she was, and she just kept on saying, "I am a Christian, and evil cannot find a place among us."

The Churches of Vienne and Lyons (177 A.D.)

The pain woke her out of spiritual sleep; she confessed Christ, and gladly accepted martyrdom

Now it was the turn of Sanctus to suffer again. The soldiers hoped that if they tortured him enough, he would say something incriminatory. In fact, whatever they asked him, he simply answered, "I am a Christian."

His calmness infuriated his tormentors, who then began to torture him even more sadistically. They applied red hot brass plates to the most sensitive parts of his body, so that his frame contracted under the pain and his limbs became swollen and inflamed.

A few days later they dragged him out again and began to apply their instruments of torture once again to his raw and distorted body, expecting that the pain would be so intolerable that he would at last deny Christ, or else die under the strain. Either way, they hoped that it would terrify the other Christians.

In fact, a miracle happened. As their instruments of pain touched him, his deformed frame, which had been contracted, straightened out, the swelling went down, and he regained the use of his limbs.

On the same day, one of the Christians who had, in the face of terrible threats, denied the Lord—a woman called Biblis—was brought in for torture to persuade her to produce "evidence" against her fellow-Christians. Once again there was a miracle, for the pain had the opposite effect! It appeared to wake her out of spiritual sleep, so that she not only refused to incriminate the believers, but confessed Christ herself, and gladly accepted martyrdom.

The Churches of Vienne and Lyons (177 A.D.)

To "put on Christ" is to be made a great and invincible champion

The three Christian heroes, Maturus, Sanctus and Blandina, were tested yet again at the time of the local festival, when vast crowds had gathered in the amphitheatre for the games. The two men, Maturus and Sanctus, were made to run the gauntlet of scourges and then, to the hysterical shouts of the crowd, were set upon by wild beasts. Surviving that, they were strapped in the notorious "iron chair" and slowly burnt over an open fire, making their final sacrifice as open spectacles before the world.

Blandina, who had already survived more than anyone could have imagined possible, was brought into the arena and suspended high on a wooden stake. Wild animals were then let loose around her, for whom she was intended to provide food. As she hung there, her lips moving in prayer, the Christians who were watching could not but be reminded of the One who was crucified for them, and into the fellowship of whose suffering their dear sister had entered.

In fact, not one of the wild beasts touched her, and after a while they took her down from the stake and put her back into prison. But already the courage of this small, despised, weak woman had put fresh heart in the Christians, and proved to everyone that to "put on Christ" is to be made an invincible champion.

Because of these testimonies, and others, most of those who had earlier denied Christ were born again, or their spiritual life was rekindled, so that they boldly presented themselves to the tribunal, confessing Christ, and asking that they too should be numbered with the martyrs.

And they were. Those who were Romans were beheaded. The others were given to the wild beasts. And Christ was glorified.

The Churches of Vienne and Lyons (177 A.D.)

In the bright light of this gospel morning people everywhere are waking up!

We were buried in darkness and the shadow of death, but a light shone out from heaven, purer than the sun, and everyone who opens himself to the light lives.

That darkness is the black night of sin, and that light is eternal life. The darkness cannot hold back the light, and like night giving way to the first rays of the sun, the day of the Lord has dawned. In the bright light of this gospel morning people everywhere are waking up! The dying of the night has become the resurrection of the day. That is what Paul meant by the "new creation," the dawning of another First Day.

The "sun of righteousness" shines upon every person quite impartially, just as the Father "makes his sun rise on good and bad alike." All are flooded with the light of truth, though not all receive it.

And all of this comes from Christ himself, the Light of the world, who by dying crucified death, and by his resurrection changed the setting into a rising sun, the blackness of night into the radiance of the morning.

Clement of Alexandria (155-220 A.D.)

Ours is a covenant of faith and hope and confidence

May I give you a piece of advice, and urge it on you? And remember, I'm speaking to you as a friend, as someone just like yourselves, not some superior religious teacher! I love each one of you more than I love my own life. So please take what I am saying very seriously.

I am concerned about an unhealthy emphasis that has led some of you astray. It springs from the misleading idea that the "Jews' Covenant" applies to Christians as well, and that therefore we are bound by all the laws and regulations of the Jewish religion. This, in turn, has led to some people exaggerating their own sins, almost glorying in their failure!

However, in one sense, the Jews' Covenant *is* for Christians. After all, the Jews themselves rejected it almost before Moses had received it. By the time he had climbed down the mountain with the tables of stone, they had broken the very laws God had just given. Moses understood the significance of that, and smashed the tables of stone to pieces. That covenant of theirs was smashed with the broken tables, so that the covenant God would make through Jesus the Beloved would be worldwide.

And it is that covenant which we have entered into—not a covenant of laws and regulations and defeat, but a covenant of faith and hope and confidence.

Epistle of Barnabas (c. 120 A.D.)

...~ppen when the grace of the Spirit fills us wholly, when at the resurrection we see him face to face?

Already, here on earth, the Holy Spirit is at work in us, preparing us for immortality as we gradually open ourselves to the things of God. Wherever the Spirit of the Father dwells, there is a living person—a human body taken over by the Spirit, forgetful of itself, shaped by the Word of God. In the Spirit's strength we live the "new life", the life of obedience to the will of God. Without the Spirit of God we cannot be saved at all.

The apostle Paul called this work of the Spirit in us a "first installment," turning material beings into spiritual ones, and mortal beings into immortal ones. He does this not by getting rid of our physical bodies, of course, but by making it possible for us to share in the life of the Spirit.

Now, if the "first installment" of the Spirit brings such a sense of intimacy with God that we can call him "Abba" ("Daddy"), what will happen when the grace of the Spirit fills us wholly, when at the resurrection we see him face to face? Then we shall be made like Christ, and the Father's purpose will be perfected in us.

Irenaeus (c. 130-c. 202 A.D.)

He accepted death on behalf of the whole world, so that the whole world could be cleansed

We're all familiar with the kind of story in which some terrible disaster or calamity is averted by a hero who sacrifices himself for the common good. It may be a plague or a famine or a monster—Greek mythology is full of stories like this: the evil power is somehow placated or frustrated by the power of self-sacrifice.

Now nobody pours scorn on this idea. It's accepted in fairytales. But some people seem to find the idea of God's Son overcoming evil in real life by the power of self-sacrifice very difficult to accept.

Of course, no story involves a sacrifice like Christ's. He accepted death on behalf of the whole world, so that the whole world could be cleansed—a world that was doomed to perish. Jesus alone, by his divine power, was able to take on himself the burden of the sins of the world. He carried it to the cross where he offered himself as a sacrifice for our sins. Like a sheep to the slaughter he humbled himself, and by his death delivered us from the peril into which our sins had put us.

Origen (c. 185-c. 254 A.D.)

The Lord chose to suffer, so that he could fulfill God's promises

How could the Lord Jesus bring himself to suffer at the hands of men? After all, he is the Lord of all the earth, the one through whom men themselves were made in God's image. Even if he was willing to suffer as a mark of his love for us, how could it happen? Would this not detract from his power and dignity?

The answer, as one would expect, is to be found in the Scriptures. The prophets, inspired by the Lord himself, foretold his coming as a man, since if he were to destroy death and bring in eternal life it was essential that he should take upon himself human flesh. And to take on human flesh involves suffering: the two are virtually indistinguishable. Has there ever been a human being who went through life without suffering?

But it was not just a matter of accepting the inevitable. The Lord *chose* to suffer, so that he could fulfil God's promises to our ancestors by revealing the depth of his love for them, suffering and dying for us and then raising us as he was raised, drawing together a new people of God.

And the clearest evidence of the extent of that love is his choice of the apostles. Rather than choose only the reliable, the honest and the dependable, he went for some men who were unstable and even dishonest. As he said himself, he did not come to call saints, but sinners.

Epistle of Barnabas (c. 120 A.D.)

The Knowledge of Good and Evil

Our duty is to learn obedience on earth, so that one day ~~u~~
glory in heaven

When man received the knowledge of good and evil, his mind could distinguish right from wrong, so that he was called upon to make a choice.

This had a good effect, because he could never really appreciate what was good without knowing what was bad. Experience could teach him the difference in a way that theory could never have done.

After all, it's by experience that the tongue tells the difference between what is bitter and what is sweet. It's by experience that the eye tells the difference between black and white, and the ear learns to distinguish one musical note from another. In just the same way the mind learns the difference between good and evil.

The first lesson is the result of disobedience—that disobeying God always brings evil and bitter consequences. The second lesson is the blessing of obedience, with its consequences in goodness and joy.

The process is straightforward—we cannot become immortal until we have experienced mortality; we cannot become perfect unless we have experienced imperfection. Our duty is to learn obedience on earth, so that one day we can enjoy glory in heaven.

Irenaeus (c. 130-c. 202 A.D.)

Those of us who have found our place in his perfect plan... know how profound that peace is

A quiet, inward peace of mind: that must be our goal. After all, it was God's original plan for his children.

Look at him, our Father and our Creator, and see in him all those priceless and incomparable gifts of peace. The eyes of faith will note his inexhaustible patience, his infinite calm; and that in the whole vast complex of his creation there is not a single discordant note.

The heavens revolve at his command, and do so in silent submission. Day silently gives way to night, night silently yields to day. The sun, the moon and the stars with infinite calm move without a sound along their appointed orbits. Vegetation springs up out of the soil, to provide food for people and animals. Silently, in the depths of the sea, his law still rules; and silently it rules in the caverns and chasms of the earth.

And look at the harmony of what he has made; the intricate combination of seasons, winds, rains. The most minute creature, the tiniest plant—each plays its part in his plan of peace and harmony, a plan designed by him for the good of all men.

And it is those of us who have found *our* place in his perfect plan—that place of mercy in our Lord Jesus—who should know better than anyone else how profound that peace is, how perfect that harmony.

Clement of Rome (30-100 A.D.)

In all your activities, make the gospel of the Lord Jesus Christ your only and absolute guide

On Sunday, the Lord's Day, all the Christians should come to-gether to break bread and give thanks. But this should not be done casually or without preparation.

For instance, you should not take part in this service if you have any misunderstanding with one of your fellow-Christians. That would be to make the offering of worship impure—even profane. The Lord had told us that true worship should be an "undefiled sacrifice." So all such differences and grievances must be settled before we can offer pure worship.

Before coming to the Lord's table we should also confess our sins and faults, open and secret, so that they may be forgiven and we can draw near with clean hearts. If it is necessary to reprove one another over some fault or other, make sure that you do it in a gentle, loving way, not angrily or maliciously. Do it in the spirit of the Gospel.

But have nothing to do with anyone who has caused pain or hurt to his neighbor. Until he repents, you should exclude him from the fellowship.

In short, in your prayers, in your giving and in all your ac-tivities, make the Gospel of the Lord Jesus Christ your only and absolute guide.

It leads from wrong attitudes to wrong behavior, and ends in utter destruction

The way of darkness is the way of death, for it destroys men's souls. Those who follow it give to things God has made the honor due to him alone. They are self-important, belligerent and arrogant. They love power, and in pursuit of it will engage in any kind of sharp practice or deceit. They treat God's gift of sex as a plaything and his gift of life itself as subject to their whims—indeed, they casually destroy babies (born or unborn) as though they were not made in the image of God. The things they value most are in fact valueless; their sole ambition is to promote their own interests.

They are utterly indifferent to any pleas to help the poor, the deprived or the handicapped, closing their ears to such pleas. Because they hate the truth and detest goodness, they go out of their way to make life difficult for those who follow Christ and obey God's laws. They do the devil's work, and inevitably that means that some of them get caught up in the devil's own religion, sorcery, and black magic.

Beware of the way of darkness. It leads from wrong attitudes to wrong behavior and ends in utter destruction and God's judgment.

Be generous to others, and you will soon find out how generous God can be with his rewards

On the way of light, your travelling companion is your brother. You are on your way home together. So do not call what you carry with you on the journey your own. Share it with him, as one day you will share heaven with him.

Be slow to speak. Hasty words often wound. They are a snare both for those who hear them and those who speak them.

Don't be one of those whose hands are quick to grab but slow to give. And cherish, as the apple of your eye, those who preach the Word of the Lord to you.

Keep the day of judgment in mind all the while. It will sharpen your determination to work for God, either by the words you speak, or by the effort of your hands.

Be generous to others, and you will soon find out how generous God can be with his rewards. Hold the faith without denying any of it nor adding to it. Confess your faults, so that you can pray with a clear conscience.

That is the way of light.

Epistle of Barnabas (c. 120 A.D.)

*We are more delighted in something we have regained than if we had
never lost it!*

It is surprising, but true, that we are more jubilant at the conversion of a really bad person to Christ than of one who has lived a
comparatively good life. But is it so surprising? Isn't there a fun-
damental truth about life here?

After all, the Father in heaven rejoices over the one sinner
who repents rather than over the ninety-nine just people who do
not need to repent. We read in the words of Christ how the
shepherd carries home the sheep that had been lost, rejoicing,
and also how the father of the prodigal son rejoiced because his
son "was dead, yet is alive again; was lost, yet is found."

So what a truth is this, that we are more delighted in something we have regained than if we had never lost it!

Augustine of Hippo (354-430 A.D.)

His rewards are for servants who actually serve, and followers who actually follow

God did not make the first man because he needed company, but because he wanted someone to whom he could show his generosity and love.

God did not tell us to follow him because he needed our help but because he knew that serving him would make us whole.

Our work for God—our service—adds nothing to his power or his achievements. He does not *need* anything we can give him, not even our obedience.

But that does not mean that our work and service for him is meaningless or without value. God has promised to those who serve and follow him life, immortality and eternal glory. These rewards are specifically for servants who actually *serve*, and followers who actually *follow*. Their service and their following please him and enrich them, but God himself derives no other advantage from them, because he is complete in himself and lacks nothing.

Irenaeus (c. 130-c. 202 A.D.)

He ascended to heaven openly, so that he could come back to us inwardly, and never leave us again

The contentment which you seek depends entirely upon God. There is no satisfaction where you are seeking it, in self-indulgence and the unrewarding pleasures of the body. By all means seek contentment and satisfaction, but start looking for them somewhere real. At present you are looking for a happy life in what is, to all intents and purposes, a graveyard. You can't find a happy life where there's no life at all!

The one true life came down to earth and died for us, destroying death by swamping it with his own life. And with a voice of thunder he now invites us to return to him. He shared our mortal life on earth, and now calls us to share his eternal life in heaven. That is contentment.

Where can we find him? Not on earth, for he is not here. And not in heaven, for we are not there. But in our own hearts we can find him. He ascended to heaven openly so that he could come back to us inwardly, and never leave us again.

Augustine of Hippo (354-430 A.D.)

It is not our holiness, but his, given to us through the power of the Holy Spirit as he works in us

There would be no need for the Holy Spirit if we could become holy in our own strength, but God has sent him to our aid because we can't. We derive our existence from the Father; the Son, the "Word", reveals the truth to our minds, and the Holy Spirit makes us holy.

It is when the Holy Spirit has worked in us, making holy what was before unclean, that we can go on to receive God's righteousness in Christ. That is to say, it is not our holiness, but his, given to us through the power of the Spirit as he works in us, and it makes possible that true and deep understanding of God's ways and purposes which we call "wisdom."

So the believer is intended to make progress, to grow. The Father gives natural life to everybody, but his purpose for us is so much more than that. He wishes us to go on to share more and more fully in Christ's righteousness, understanding and wisdom. Eventually—as the Holy Spirit cleanses and purifies us—all the stains of human sin and ignorance are removed and the being made by God becomes worthy of God.

Then, and only then, is human destiny fulfilled. God gave us life for this purpose—that we might be perfect, as he is perfect.

Origen (c. 185-c. 254 A.D.)

You are the only friend who never goes away

No matter in which direction we turn for satisfaction (other than towards you, Lord) it will lead to pain—not at once, but eventually. The object of our devotion may be good and pure and beautiful . . . but it is nothing apart from you.

Every object of beauty has its spring and its fall. It begins its life in the spring, grows to perfection of form and beauty, and then grows old and withers away. The more speedily it advances to perfection, the more speedily it comes to an end.

This impermanence is part of your divine plan, to show us that even the loveliest and best things in creation are not complete in themselves. They are part of the whole creation, and by withering and passing away they make room for other creatures which are to follow.

So, Lord, deliver me from exaggerated love of any of your creatures, for by their nature they come and go, moving irreversibly to their end, yet tearing our affections apart with desires that can never be fulfilled.

Man's spirit longs to commit itself to what it loves, but it cannot commit itself to your creatures, because, instead of remaining, they fly away.

But no one loses you, Lord. You do not change. You have no fall, no winter, no beginning, no ending. You are the only friend who never goes away.

Augustine of Hippo (354-430 A.D.)

They had what you most admired, and what they had came from Christ

It is not our task to argue people into the kingdom, nor to use methods of persuasion favored by the world. Christ taught us how to lead people gently and patiently from the love of evil to the love of God.

You must have seen this method in action—I expect many of you yourselves were drawn to him in this way. You were violent, perhaps, or inconsistent, or dishonest, or bent on revenge if you were wronged.

But you noticed that Christians had different attitudes. Their lives were consistent and reliable in all circumstances. When they were defrauded or wronged, they accepted it with amazing calmness. And when you did business with them, you were astonished at their honesty and fair dealing.

And it was *that* that convinced you, wasn't it? The sheer quality of the lives they lived as your neighbors, friends or colleagues overcame every objection. they had what you most admired, and what they had came from Christ. It was what they did, rather than what they said, that led you to him.

Justin (c. 100-165 A.D.)

...., ...rit of truth can refresh us with pure water

God gave breath to the first man to bring his whole body to life, and he has given his new "breath," the Holy Spirit, to the Church, for the same purpose—that every member of the body should come alive. The Spirit is our link with Christ. He strengthens our faith, he gives eternal life, and he is a ladder by which we can come to God.

All the means through which the Holy Spirit works are within the Church—that is why the Church is a living body. "God has set apostles, prophets and teachers in the Church," the apostle Paul says, and they are channels of the Spirit.

Where the Church is, there is the Spirit of God. And where the Spirit is, there is the Church, and every kind of grace.

But the Spirit is also truth. He cannot operate through a lie. So those who seek the Spirit but deny the truth are trying to draw water from leaking reservoirs—and they will pollute the water, too. Only the Spirit of truth can refresh us with pure water, the water of life that flows from Christ into his people.

Irenaeus (c. 130-c. 202 A.D.)

Even if it offends our relatives and friends, shouldn't we do what is right, and what will bring us to God?

"Don't ask me to change my way of life," you say. "It's unreasonable to expect me to welcome having my routine turned upside down. In any case, I'm satisfied with my own ways—that's how I was brought up. I don't see any *need* to change!"

All right, let's accept your argument. You were brought up on milk. Why then have you "changed" to a new diet? You spent the first years of your life clinging to your mother. Why have you let go of her? And when you travel, do you always follow the same route? It's safer, of course—but a bit boring!

So, if the old way, your present way of life, is unsatisfactory—if it ignores God, or disturbs your conscience—wouldn't change be the best thing? Even if it offends our relatives or friends, shouldn't we do what is right, and what will bring us to the truth and to God? Isn't it possible that tradition, custom, a comfortable "rut," a familiar life-style, may keep us from the greatest thing life offers? And if so, isn't custom a deadly drug, tranquilizing us, preventing changes that will be wholly for the good?

Clement of Alexandria (155-220 A.D.)

The Christian God fills heaven and earth, and those who believe can worship him anywhere

For breaking a decree ordering everyone to make sacrifices to idols, several leading Christians, led by Justin, were arrested and brought before the Prefect of Rome, Rusticus.

Rusticus: What beliefs do you follow?

Justin: We believe in the Christian God, the one God who has existed from the beginning, the Maker and Designer of the whole creation, visible and invisible. And we believe in the Lord Jesus Christ, the Son of God, who was foretold by the prophets as the one who was to come to declare salvation and lead his followers to the truth. And we don't believe this as a matter of human opinion, but as something revealed by God and confirmed by prophecy.

Rusticus: Where is your meeting place?

Justin: Anywhere and everywhere—we meet wherever we can. The Christian God is not confined to any one place. He fills heaven and earth, and those who believe can worship him anywhere.

Our real father is Christ, and our real mother is our faith in him

Rusticus:	Where does this group of disciples meet?
Justin:	I'm staying in Martin's house—I have an upstairs room. That's near the Baths of Timothy. This is my second visit to Rome, and so far as I know the Christians have always met in his home. But if people seeking the truth came to me, I would meet them in my room.
Rusticus:	So you don't deny that you are a Christian?
Justin:	No. I am a Christian.
Rusticus:	And you others, are you all Christians?
The Others:	We are, by God's gift.
Rusticus:	And did Justin convert you to Christianity?
Paeon:	No. I received the truth from my parents.
Euelpistus:	So did I, though I was glad to learn more from Justin.
Rusticus:	Where are your parents?
Euelpistus:	In Cappadocia.
Hierax:	Our real father is Christ, and our real mother is our faith in him. My earthly parents are dead. I was brought from Iconium as a captive.
Rusticus:	And you—what do you say? Are you an unbeliever like the rest of them?
Liberian:	Not an "unbeliever." I am a Christian. I believe in and love the only true God. That is not "unbelief."

We would rather suffer now and please the Lord, than please you and suffer on that day

The Prefect, Rusticus, now turned his attention to Justin.

Rusticus: You are supposed to be an intelligent man, and you claim that you know the "truth," as you call it. Now tell me, if I order you to be beaten and then beheaded, do you really and truly believe you will go up to heaven?

Justin: If I endure these things—if I don't deny Christ—then I expect to receive his gift of eternal life. That is the promise of God to all who live in him, until the end of the age.

Rusticus: You think you will go to heaven then?

Justin: I don't *think*, I know it. I'm totally persuaded.

Rusticus: Ah well, let's turn our attention to a more urgent question. Will you all agree to make a sacrifice to the Roman gods?

Justin: No one in his right mind turns from true belief to false.

Rusticus: If you refuse to sacrifice, you will all be punished without mercy.

Justin: There is an even more terrible seat of judgment than a Roman Prefect's, the judgment seat of our Lord, who will one day judge the whole world. We would rather suffer now and please him, than please you and suffer then. You must do whatever you decide. We are Christians, and we do not sacrifice to idols.

The Christians were then led out, and beheaded, glorifying God and confessing Christ.

The choice is between our own private good and pleasing you, who are the common Good of all

We fall into sin when we turn from you, the Fountain of life, the Maker and Ruler of all things. To cut ourselves off from life, creation and order is to invite failure.

But we also fall into sin when we confuse a part for the whole—when through desire or pride or folly we get things out of perspective and come to value one thing (a relationship, perhaps, or an ambition) more highly than we value our total life and our total good.

Yet when we have sinned, for these or any other reasons, we can return, we can come back to you, with humility (because we have failed and are failures) and with new devotion (because you do not change). And when we do, you cleanse us from the sin, and from its effects. More than that, if we sincerely desire it, you "hear the groans of the prisoners" and release us from the chains we have made for ourselves. So that, provided we do not deliberately set out to flaunt our freedom, you will keep us from doing it again.

Generally, we must choose between our own private good—wanting to please ourselves; or wanting to please you, who are the common Good of all.

Augustine of Hippo (354-430 A.D.)

The battlefield is now fertile land on which we cultivate love

We have been completely changed. Formerly our minds were obsessed with violence. Our one aim was to out-do the other man, whatever the cost. Life was little more than a battlefield for our ambition and our greed.

But now the weapons of that "war" have been transformed. As the prophet foresaw, we have beaten our swords into ploughshares, and the battlefield is now fertile land on which we cultivate love of God, love of man, faith and hope—all of them gifts of the Father through the One who was crucified.

Each of us "dwells under his own vine," as the Psalmist envisioned it. Our homes are happy, our marriages secure, our lives contented.

Justin (c. 100-165 A.D.)

When you "behead" the vine it does not die, but bursts out in other, fruit-bearing branches

It is true that there is violence in the Christian life, but now it is done to us, not by us. Because of our faith we are crucified, beheaded, fed to wild beasts or burned in the flames. By these means, some hope to persuade us to deny Christ. They intend to wipe out the Church.

But their persecution has had the opposite effect! Think of that "vine" again. When you "behead" it—pruning away some branches—it does not die, but bursts out in other, fruit-bearing branches. That is what happens with us. What others intend for destruction is turned to growth. Unbelievers see this invincible faith, and become believers in the Name of Jesus.

After all, he himself spoke of this vine, planted by God, rooted in Christ. It is his people.

Justin (c. 100-165 A.D.)

Our friend will rise, not with tears of dismay but with splendor and glory

When a dear one dies, the unbeliever sees a cadaver, but the Christian sees a body asleep. The unbeliever says that the dead person has "gone." We agree, but we remember *where* he has gone. He has gone where the apostle Paul is, where Peter is, where the whole company of the saints are. We remember that he will rise, not with tears of dismay, but with splendor and glory.

So why should we mourn like unbelievers when, in every respect, our position is the opposite of theirs? To give in to grief and despair cannot alter what has happened or bring back the loved one who has died, and if persisted in it may damage our own personalities. We should not imitate those who have no hope. "Do not sorrow," Paul tells us, *"as do those who have no hope."* For we have hope. That is the simple difference between us!

John Chrysostom (347-407 A.D.)

None of us has yet attained perfection. We all still need to grow

It is one thing to have confidence in God, but quite another to be overconfident in yourself. There is a danger that those who believe themselves to be among "the chosen" may adopt a smug, self-confident attitude, withdrawing into themselves and feeling superior to the people around them, as though they had already won God's final seal of approval.

    If you are tempted to think like that, remember what Isaiah says: "Shame on you who are wise in your own eyes, and knowledgeable in your own esteem." None of us has yet attained perfection. We all still need to grow. So come and take your full share in our gatherings and in our discussions, which are aimed at helping all of us towards maturity. Don't stand aloof, as though you knew it all already!

It is a path on which none need stumble, and which finally leads men home

There are two ways of living, under two sources of power. One is the way of light, the other the way of darkness. The first way is lit by the angels of God; the second is overshadowed by the angels of Satan.

The way of light is not easy. The pilgrim along this road will find his journey home is a hard and long one. But to help him on his way the Lord has set many lights and many signposts.

The lights are the love of the Creator who made him, the power of the Lord of the earth, the glory of the Redeemer who conquered death.

The signposts are ways to follow: singleness of heart; richness of spirit; the rejection of hypocrisy and separation from those who are walking the way of death.

In short, the way of light is the way of God's commandments. Follow them, respect them, obey them and you will find it a path on which none need stumble, and which finally leads men home.

Epistle of Barnabas (c. 120 A.D.)

There is always the greater joy where the greater fear precedes it

The world is full of examples of the joy that flows from pain, effort and loss. The army general is always pleased to win a battle, but the harder the fight, the greater his satisfaction in victory. Passengers are always glad to arrive safely at their destination, but how much more delighted they are to arrive when there has been some danger during the journey! And aren't we all more glad to see a friend up and about again after a serious illness than we were when he was fit and well—even if he never regains his old strength?

It seems that this part of God's creation consists as it were of risings and fallings, of hatreds and reconciliations, of fears and deliverances. And there is always the greater joy where the greater fear preceded it.

So it is with Christ who died and rose, who came down and ascended, who shared our great sorrow and leads us to the greatest joy.

Augustine of Hippo (354-430 A.D.)

We can see the glory of the Lord Christ in every earthly kingdom

Think for a moment how universal the sign of the cross is, how closely it is connected with every aspect of life. Take the mast of a ship, for example—the cross formed by the yardarm is like a symbol of victory as it drives ahead through stormy seas. Ploughs and spades have this cross shape. Man himself is distinguished from animals by standing upright and being able to extend his arms like a cross.

And the symbols of power in our society—how profoundly the idea of the cross is expressed through them! When the Roman legions march behind their ensigns they are in fact marching under the cross, and when victory poles are carried, the victory they remind us of is the victory of the cross.

So, if we wish, we can see the Lord Christ in everything: his victory in every human symbol, his glory in every earthly kingdom, his sign in every heathen inscription.

Justin (c. 100-165 A.D.)

In that action one who fulfilled the law justified millions who broke it

Earlier in our lives, God allowed us to be dominated by our uncontrolled impulses. He didn't do this because he in any way approved of our sins, or regarded them as insignificant or temporary.

His motive was quite different. He wanted us to experience the darkness of sin before he showed us the light of holiness. He wanted us to see how bankrupt our own efforts were, how incapable of bringing us to life, before (through his own kindness) he made us what we could never make ourselves.

But once we had seen clearly that we could never earn entry into the kingdom of God, he gave it us as a gift! Our sins excluded us, but he took them from us and gave his own Son as a ransom for us. Christ's righteousness covered our sins. The perfect Son of God took our place—the lawbreakers, the blasphemers.

What a beautiful exchange that was! What an act of creation beyond human understanding, for in that action one who was good covered millions who were evil, and one who fulfilled the law justified millions who broke it!

Epistle to Diognetus (c. 150 A.D.)

Our Father loves to share his generosity through us with everybody

If someone strikes you on the right cheek, turn the other cheek to him. If someone makes you go a mile, go two with him. If someone takes your coat, offer him your shirt as well. If someone seizes something that belongs to you, let it go (you couldn't get it back, anyway!). Give to everyone who asks and don't expect to be paid back. Our Father loves to share his generosity through us with everybody.

A generous giver is blessed by God. But the taker should beware! If he takes only what he needs, then God excuses him. But if he goes beyond that, God will require an account of why he took it, and for what purpose. In fact, he won't be let off until his actions have been minutely examined—and if he has been greedy, then he will be expected to pay back every penny.

Remember the old saying? "Keep your gifts in your own hands until you know who you are giving them to."

The Didache (c. 80 A.D.)

We should mourn for sin—but nothing else

We should thank God not only for the resurrection but also for the *hope* of it. It is that hope which comforts us in the face of bereavement and helps us to think of those who have died with courage, and even joy. We know they will rise again, and that we shall meet them.

If we must sorrow, don't let us waste our sorrow on *them*! Let's sorrow for those who live in sin, not for those who die in faith. The apostle Paul once spoke of those for whom he mourned—not those who had died, but those who were alive and had not repented of their sins. Of course, we shall—and we should—weep a little for those who have left us, even though we know we shall see them again. But we should weep far more for the folly of the sinner.

So let us be selective in our mourning. Let us get our priorities in order. We should mourn for our sin, but for nothing else that comes to us—not poverty, nor sickness, nor injustice, nor abuse, nor untimely death. Whatever human trial comes our way, let us bear it without resentment. We may well find that these calamities add, not to our tears, but to our crowns.

John Chrysostom (347-407 A.D.)

Every experience and every relationship that comes our way is to be accepted as a blessing

Bring up your children from their earliest days to respect holy things and reverence God, and if they need correction, do not be afraid to punish them.

Don't waste your energy trying to compete with your neighbor and reject every temptation to envy him his possessions. Don't set yourself material goals, or set your heart on cultivating friendships with those who are rich and famous. It is far better to spend your time with those who are modest and good-living people. But every experience and every relationship that comes our way is to be accepted as a blessing, because nothing can happen to us without God's permission.

At work, be polite to your employer, seeing him too as an instrument of God's purpose. At the same time, when it is your turn to give orders, deal in a kind and generous manner with your subordinates. If you are aggressive or unpleasant, they will not only lose their respect for you but also, knowing you are a Christian, may lose their respect for God. In any case, the Lord did not come to earth to call people according to their rank or social status. The only "qualification" that impresses him is the mark of the Holy Spirit, who prepares us for heaven.

Epistle of Barnabas (c. 120 A.D.)

All things are, of themselves, good; but everything is not good for everybody

I looked at the created things around me, and saw that every one of them owed its very existence to you, Lord. And I saw that every finite thing is "in" you, but not in the usual meaning of that word "in." They are not in you in the sense of their location (that is, inside you); but in you in the sense that they are contained in reality, they really exist—and you are the only guarantee of existence, because you alone exist in your own right.

But though this told me that all things are, of themselves, good, because they are in you, I also found by experience that everything is not good for everybody.

Bread is good, and to a man with a healthy palate it tastes good, too. But to a man who is sick the same good bread may taste repulsive.

Light is good. But the sunlight which delights healthy eyes causes pain and distress to a person with sore or sensitive eyes.

Your justice is good. To the righteous man it is a delight. But by the same token, to those who disobey you that very justice is a deeply offensive, even terrifying, thing.

Augustine of Hippo (354-430 A.D.)

Love is stronger than death"—so practice kindness

Christ was kind, courteous and thoughtful to poor people as well as rich ones, to "nobodies" as well as the famous. So when you are in a position to do someone a kindness, don't miss the golden opportunity. After all, "love is stronger than death."

Be meticulous in regard to the rights of others, including unbelievers, so that they cannot criticize your consistent manner of life. In that way, the Church will win the approval of those outside, and the Lord's name will be honored rather than brought into disrepute. It is, of course, a deadly serious matter when you bring dishonor on his name, so impress upon yourselves how important this is.

Polycarp of Smyrna (c. 69-155 A.D.)

When we grow weary of trying to prove ourselves, we may be ready to cast ourselves upon him

"The Word was made flesh" so that the wisdom of God could come within the reach of human beings. For his Word—the expression of the whole truth about God—is far beyond our comprehension. No creature can ever fully understand his creator. But the Word, the Son of God, put on a humble, human form, so that infinite truth could be seen in finite terms.

He humbled himself, coming down to the lowest human level. Those who will join him there—denying themselves, taking the low place—will be raised up with him to the heights of heaven.

It is not easy for man to stoop so low, or to abandon his self-confidence. But when he sees the divine Son lying, as it were, at his feet, wrapped in the clothes of human poverty, then his heart may be moved and his pride cured. And when we grow weary of trying to prove ourselves, we may be ready to cast ourselves upon him.

When we do, he who came down to where we are raises us to where he is.

Augustine of Hippo (354-430 A.D.)

The death of sin removes the darkness, the disappointment and the defeat

There was a time when I felt my life was a prison in which I was trapped. I was so deeply in the grip of my own failure that I could not believe that I would ever escape from it. I literally despaired of any improvement, let alone release.

And then it happened! Light from heaven shone into my heart. My old life was washed away and a new life, the life of the Spirit of God, was born in me. I became a new person.

And straight away doubts began to be resolved. Closed doors began to open, giving my life a freedom, a vision it had lacked before. Dark corners were illuminated. What had seemed difficult before now seemed easy; what I had reckoned impossible was now within reach.

What I had discovered was a basic principle—that fallen human nature belongs to the earth and is prone to sin; and that redeemed human nature belongs to God and is beginning to be changed by the Holy Spirit. The death of sin removes the darkness, the disappointment, the defeat. The new life of holiness confers joy, achievement and light.

Origen (c. 185-c. 254 A.D.)

How can I lose if I commit everything to a Lover who cannot fail me?

The process of life demands that some things pass away to make room for others. The leaves fall, to be replaced, next spring, by new buds. Generation succeeds generation. Last year's dying fruit is this year's seed. It is the pattern of the creation.

But God never departs. He is outside this process. In him is a rest which cannot be disturbed, a love which lasts for ever.

So let me build my eternal home in him, and fill it with all the good things I have received from him. How can I lose if I commit everything to a Lover who cannot fail me?

And his love will bring life to all the dying parts of my soul. It will cure my moral frailty. It will take away that instability and indecision that has ruined my life.

And what is more, the weak side of my nature—the desires and passions that draw me to the passing loves and concerns of earth—will be transformed. I shall not lose my capacities to feel, to love, to enjoy, but they will serve God, not men, and bring me to salvation, not ruin.

Augustine of Hippo (354-430 A.D.)

Let us be very careful lest we are among the "many" who are "called," but not the "few" who are "chosen"

None of us has yet earned God's approval. None of us has attained perfection. The best of us are still learning; the holiest are still sinners.

So no assumption that we are among the elect should ever be allowed to undermine our efforts to make that calling and election sure. Overconfidence may simply lead us to fall asleep in our sins, and give the devil a chance to gain control of our minds and attitudes.

Israel was chosen. Signs, miracles and wonders were performed for her. And yet she was rejected through unbelief. Let us be very careful lest we are among the "many" who are "called," but not the "few" who are "chosen."

A healthy fear of God may be the best guard against presumption

There is something repulsive about boasting of our own achievements. But that shouldn't stop us telling people about what God has done for us. That is the difference—we don't pretend it's our doing that our lives are changed, or that we can do good deeds. We make it absolutely clear that all our power for good comes from God.

And it does. He is the source of whatever spiritual life we have, and whatever spiritual strength. And he is also the source of whatever wisdom we may have. He gives us eyes that recognize the signs of the times.

There is one danger in this (other than pride, that is). Because the Lord has been so generous, and given us forgiveness andand strength, we may begin to take him for granted. A healthy fear of God may be the best guard against presumption. It will ensure that the wonderful sense of security God has given us doesn't lead to spiritual indifference.

Keep him as the guest of your soul. Then there's no chance of the old Enemy creeping in unawares and spoiling everything.

Cyprian (200-258 A.D.)

We were made in God's likeness; we are remade in the likeness of his Son

We were made "in the likeness of God." But in course of time that image has become obscured, like a face on a very old portrait, dimmed with dust and dirt.

When a portrait is spoiled, the only way to renew it is for the subject to come back to the studio and sit for the artist all over again. That is why Christ came—to make it possible for the divine image in man to be re-created. We were made in God's likeness; we are remade in the likeness of his Son.

To bring about this re-creation, Christ still comes to men and lives among them. In a special way he comes to his Church, his "body," to show us what the "image of God" is really like.

What a responsibility the Church has, to be Christ's body, showing him to those who are unable or unwilling to see him in providence, or in creation! Through the Word of God lived out in the Body of Christ they can come to the Father, and themselves be made again "in the likeness of God."

Athanasius (296-372 A.D.)

J